I L♡VE MY WIFE ~~but~~

A Husband's Guide to **Removing the But** and Embracing Your Wife's Personality as a Gift

DR. ROBERT PYLES

Copyright © 2020 Robert B. Pyles

All rights reserved. No part of this book may be reproduced or transmitted in any form or by any means without written permission from the author.

I Love My Wife, But
ISBN: 978-1-952327-14-8
Library of Congress Control Number: pending

Dedication

To my beautiful wife, Betty, there are no "buts" when loving you. Together we've built the marriage of our dreams—34 years and counting. You are my love, forever and always.

Contents

Foreword 7
Before You Begin Reading 9
Happily Ever After 13
From Dating to Distance 21
Purpose Over Problems 29
Two Personalities One Marriage 37
Honesty Heals 59
Complex Issues With Simple Solutions 77
Loving Your Wife Without the But 141
Next Steps 147

Foreword

God loves marriage, and He designed it for husbands and wives to love it as well. I believe marriage is one of the most fulfilling and rewarding relationships a man and woman can experience here on earth. Having been married over four decades, I know the gift of marrying the one God had in mind before this world began. I know what it means to grow together and to grow up together; because of this, I know how powerful a resource like this book is to a healthy marriage.

In his companion books, I Love My Wife, But and I Love My Husband, But — Pastor Pyles provides a classical compilation of truths. No matter what stage of marriage you are in, both husband and wife can grow from this work. By entering this experience with an open heart, you will discover and recover God's purpose for your union. We often forget that understanding is a core longing of every individual, especially in marriage. Pastor Pyles offers critical insights into understanding how you and your mate are uniquely wired and handknit together by God. He then challenges both husband and wife to love the personality traits that may have caused a "but" somewhere in your love walk with your mate.

For over twenty years, Pastor Pyles has been a son and a protégé of mine. I've watched his life as an innovator, trailblazer, and visionary champion of faith for his family and his community. As you read, I promise you will also grow. If you allow the anointing on this book to saturate your marital union, you will be thankful you've discovered this treasure.

My Highest Regards,

E L Warren, Ph.D
Bishop, Cathedral Of Worship
President, E L Warren Min Int
Presiding Prelate I.N.A.M
Member, Illinois State Police Merit Board
Chairman, Center for Family Preservation
Treasure International Communion Of Charismatic Churches

Before You Begin Reading

To master The Big 6, you have to be anchored in your relationships. If you are unsure of what The Big 6 is, I need you to take a moment and visit rpthebig6.com so you can learn more. The Big 6 are primary areas of your life that you must be anchored to experience exponential success. These areas are health, purpose, finances, spiritual growth, personal development, and relationships. I Love My Wife, But, will help you anchor your intimate relationship. There are follow up books to this work titled "Mastering Your Personality" volumes I and II. In each of these books, I shed light on how to understand and deal with others. It gives readers the tools for better understanding themselves and dealing with their strengths and weaknesses.

I realized that one of the most challenging places to master your personality is in personal and intimate relationships. You must understand who you are and how you're wired. Then you can understand who your partner is and how they're wired. If you don't, you will always have a but behind your love for them. That's when it hit me, "I Love My Wife, But" and the companion version, "I Love My Husband, But" It was clear to me that even loving couples married for decades were yet struggling with some of the same issues as younger couples and the newly married.

This work is personal to me because couples are essential to the family, church, and society. Families are the backbone of businesses, corporations, and governments. Couples create families, which means addressing the nature of personality must begin there. If I can help "him" be a better and more understanding husband, and if I can help "her" become a better wife, I help everything and everyone that couple is connected to become better as well.

Let's be clear.

So now that you know my purpose, let's be clear. The last thing you need is a tool to help you pick out all the negative things about your wife. On a bad day, you can do that without my help. I don't care how much in love you started out or even how much in love you are right now; the negatives can introduce themselves to you in a way that you won't forget. Call it a "pet-peeve" or whatever you wish. There are things about your wife that get on your nerves. Admit it; you will feel better.

What you really need is a tool or a way of dealing with those negative things that will help you understand her better, grow and strengthen both of you while turning any negatives into something positive for yourself. Wouldn't you like that? This book and the companion version, "I Love My Husband, But" is just the tool you need to help make that happen. It won't happen by reading alone, but you know that already. You have to commit to making changes in the way you think and react. Take the lessons and questions you read here, seriously. If you treat this process as if it's the tool you need to spark up your marriage, bring back the happiness, and fall in love all over again, that's what it will be for you.

As I share what works for me and what I would do, remember this is a process of going from where you are to where you want to be. I'm here to help you take some key steps in that direction. If you take your time and seriously work on the questions asked, do the exercises, and communicate with your mate, this tool will transform your marriage. You will remove the but and become empowered to write the book "I Love My Wife, Period."

This journey will help you. I promise. Once you receive help from this book and realize you need more – contact me at rpthebig6.com to schedule a workshop, seminar, or private coaching for you and your spouse.

Dr. Robert Pyles

Same Guy. Same Goals. Same God.

Introduction
Happily Ever After

> "Every good relationship, especially marriage, is based on respect. If it's not based on respect, nothing that appears to be good will last very long."
> **-Amy Grant**

For many of us, the decision to marry came after a series of interactions, conversations, and icebreakers, better known as dating. Believe it or not, it's on this battlefield that many of our wounded never heal, even though they go on to marriage. The reasons for this are many. One of them is a lack of respect. It sounds a little strange, but hear me out.

Going into a dating situation is challenging when you consider all the different combinations of personalities, backgrounds, and the baggage being carried. Just think of the many different possibilities. When we are dating, we often have many expectations, dreams, and hopes that we wish to fulfill. Many of these dreams and hopes come from the movie screens, romance books, and ideas in our own heads that are related to our past. This is why it is often said that no one ever dates or marries a single person. Single, meaning individual.

Many of us have the effects, hurts, and disappointments of past relationships we carry as baggage in the new or present relationship. We never date a single person simply because we have all of the other people and experiences in our history. Since they have not been laid to rest, they are alive and well to influence your present thoughts and dreams, even when it comes to relationships or marriage.

Somewhere inside all of us is a small but powerful voice. This voice speaks up when it looks like our painful past is trying to get back into our future. Out of the past trauma and hurt, memories surface, pain is remembered, and that is when the voice speaks. Out of fear of the past coming back, it says, "I'm not going to let that happen to me again!" So, we make sure that we watch for the signs and throw out a test or two, always testing and remaining insecure while wanting to be loved, but not sure if you can fully trust the lover. It is for this reason that many of us have decided to take care of number one. "After all, no one else is going to take care of me or fight for me; I have to." Carrying that hurt and mistrust into a relationship, we become selfish and think of what we want.

Many of us started dating with only one thing in mind, what would be pleasing to US. We didn't stop to think about the other person. We had an idea in mind, and we wanted it to be fulfilled. To put it differently, as quiet as it is kept, you wanted her to be petite with 36, 24, 36, coke-bottle shape. Perhaps you wanted someone that looks like a movie star you have watched parade across your screen. Maybe you remember one of the best relationships you had in the past, and wanted her to be like your lost love, and so you required her to have some of the same similarities and characteristics. Psychologically, mentally, or however you want to put it, you are loving an old lover while embracing your mate. That is scary.

You may not realize it, but you are living in the past. I know you would never say it out loud but, your hidden and secret desire is to love a ghost in your past rather than the dedicated person that stands before you. You see her through a lens colored with many faces and feelings from your past. Tell me, did you choose her because of who she was, or is she just a collection of all the good pieces of other lovers from your past?

> *Many times, we don't know what we want, we only want what we've known.*

Even if you are fortunate enough to know what you want, sometimes what you want comes with unrealistic motivations. This is selfishness that causes the person to pick and choose not out of reality but more like a Hollywood styled fairytale of romance. As we will discuss later, many have delusions about dating and relationships. It's this person who wakes up later only to ask, "What was I thinking, how did I ever marry this person?"

There are many answers to that question. One answer most certainly is selfish motivations. I'll explain it. Ask any of your brothers and friends what their criteria would be for choosing the perfect mate, or the perfect date. And you will begin to hear things like, "She has to be fine, independent, nice shape with long hair, and so on…" Does this sound familiar to you? What were you shopping for? Was your list the same as the one above?

Here's why lists like this are selfish. A person may have all of these things and also may have extra baggage that you wouldn't want to carry. The things that make a lasting relationship and marriage have nothing to do with height, complexion, large bank accounts, the kind of car she drives, and so on. Just ask the man who always gets his way but is living lonely in marriage. He is not happy and feels trapped, realizing he is alone, sleeping with a stranger while being a stranger to the one he is intimate with —his wife. Those who have been around the block a few times have updated their list to reflect the truth. What is needed is truth, honesty, and a compassionate, considerate, loving, kind soul to walk hand in hand with till death parts you and her.

You know that love comes from the inside out, and so should the interest in dating and getting to know the other person. Selfishness begins to rule the relationship when one decides what the other better have or better do for them. This breeds a lack of respect because the other person's mind, heart, and soul are out of the picture. All that is seen is what you want and had better get, and those things don't make for a lasting and loving marriage if they are absent of the other things I mentioned above. Were you looking for someone loving and compassionate, considerate, God-fearing, and kind? Or was your first item, her shape, hair length, complexion, face, ability to support you, and so on?

Let's Go Deeper

You are reading this book because you want a better marriage, a better relationship, or a desire to make the right choices before choosing altogether. This means that you see a need to improve your present or future situation by starting with you. That is a good place to start.

Think back over your past dating or marital history. How have things been? Think about the women you've dated in the past and even the outcome of the relationship or relationships. Do you see a pattern?

Warning! As you look and try to find a pattern, stay away from generalizations like, "Yes I see a pattern, all women cheat, all women are gold-diggers, and all women want is money." If you feel that way, you may want to find a counselor or therapist, really. Take a look at your pattern. Do you have a habit of falling in love too quickly or not trusting as you should? Do you always seem to choose the "wrong" person, or find a good woman but somehow end up losing her?

Maybe even now, you are wondering about your present situation. To keep it "real," it's a little late in the game to ask why you have chosen the mate that you have if you have one. If you feel you have been handed a lemon of a relationship, it is time to decide to make lemonade or lemon meringue pie.

Stop asking questions like, "What is wrong with her?" and begin to ask the deeper question. What is the deeper question? It might go something like this, "Rather than trying to make her see things my way, have I really tried to understand her?" "Am I assuming that I know all that I need to about her, am I taking her for granted?"

You may think she is complicated or too much to deal with. However, you could be the cause of some of your problems with her. You should think of her reactions as a response to her environment. Think about it. You give her groceries; she makes it a meal. You give her a house; she makes it a home. You give her seed; she shapes it and delivers you a living child. Your wife is a master at taking what you give her and bringing it to its next level of expression. This includes what you give her by way of emotions, habits, and problems. This is not to say that everything is your fault because it isn't. However, you will find that she is largely responding to what you have provided—junk in, junk out.

> *There is a good chance that the "negative" you see are a reaction to your behavior.*

Did you know?

"In the United States, researchers estimate that 40%–50% of all first marriages, and 60% of second marriages, will end in divorce. There are some well-known factors that put people at higher risk for

divorce: marrying at a very early age, less education and income, living together before marriage, a premarital pregnancy, no religious affiliation, coming from a divorced family, and feelings of insecurity. The most common reasons people give for their divorce are lack of commitment, too much arguing, infidelity, marrying too young, unrealistic expectations, lack of equality in the relationship, lack of preparation for marriage, and abuse." [1]

I want to challenge you to deepen your commitment. You will find questions that will help you to uncover hidden truths about marriage and the one you have chosen as your life partner. Along the way, you will realize that you are not crazy, but rather there are good reasons why you seem to butt heads, disagree, or even rub each other the wrong way. You will discover why you have those feelings of not being able to stand her sometimes, and why you love her more than anything other times. When you understand personality, it gives you a deeper understanding of why things are the way they are. You need to understand her personality and yours, and vice versa. When you understand this, it begins to chip away at the "but" until there is only "love." Remember, this book is a companion series that addresses husbands and wives, so be sure that everything you'll read, she will too. If you want to know what I'm sharing with her, grab the companion book once you're **done** exploring your role in loving her more.

I encourage husbands and wives to read the book together, talk about it, embrace it together. Complete the exercises without judgment of each other. Be honest and patient, after all, the rest of your life is a long time to live incomplete and unfulfilled – especially in your marriage. The strategies that help remove the *but* from our relationships are centered on mastering your personality. To learn more about this stay connected for my fall 2020 book release that will go even deeper into this topic.

Together we will unpack personality types that I describe as Earth, Air, Water, and Fire. Each type relates to the well-known D.I.S.C. personality assessments and the Jungian Type Personality Index of Choleric, Melancholy, Sanguine, and Phlegmatic. I'll describe my interpretation of the personality temperaments and encourage you to do ongoing learning about your personality and temperament through one of the mentioned philosophies.

I believe that professional counseling is not only meaningful but also necessary. So, as you are reading this book, if you identify that you need another level of care, I recommend you seek out a professional caregiver or therapist. This book is to empower you to love your spouse well and to empower them to love you well. This love is based on how you are wired and what you need. If each person in the marriage is focused on meeting the other person's needs, both needs are met, and the marriage is successful.

Chapter 1
From Dating to Distance

"If God is going to write your love story, He's going to first need your pen."
-Eric Ludy

As a man, you know you are very different than every woman you meet. While a girl is developing into a woman, she thinks of her life as a woman with one man. When boys continue to grow, they usually can't imagine being married; you are too focused on winning the attention of more than one girl or young lady. As time moves on, many men become less and less excited about committed relationships and marriage. Truth is, it's just too easy to get what today's woman is so easily giving away, sex.

There are many married men today that started out wondering if they would ever marry. Like the song said, "I fooled around and fell in love..." Some wanted to continue being a "playah-playah," and others got tired of playing and being played. Like the movie "Boomerang," starring Eddie Murphy and Vivica Foxx, where Eddie Murphy ends up being treated exactly as he had treated scores of women. Only then does he understand the reality of what he's done.

Maybe you had a similar situation where you either got what you deserved or just never had the heart to be a dog (treat women like objects and not like the beautiful gifts they are). Since you didn't want to be like others that you saw, you decided to be a good man and treat your woman right. You started dating.

Trying to attract the right woman, you were busy. You made sure you were dressed sharp as a tack, wanting to attract the right kind of woman, you made sure your hair was combed, nails clean, and your shoes shined. Sure, some days, you went for the rugged look, but when you wanted to attract, you knew just how to charm the ladies. When you wanted to, you knew how to turn heads. It didn't matter if it was working your greatest assets like your smile, your physique, or your personality.

One day, you saw "Her." And just like you wanted, "She" saw you. You found your way through the rough and rocky waters of getting through the beginning stages. You asked all the right questions and found out whether she still lived with her parents, had or didn't have a job, and whether or not she had good credit. After that, you checked for the obvious, "How does she treat her father, are we compatible, or even, are those her mother's hips in the making?"

After doing the "research," you were pleased to find out she had decent credit (better than yours at least), a good head on her shoulders, her mother's hips, and a faithful workout schedule. Realizing there was potential and that you've talked with her enough to know she wouldn't embarrass you around your family and friends, you were happy to progress to the next step · seeing if she could cook without the words "instant" or "heat and serve."

Having crossed all the bridges and moved through the hard spots, you and she fell in love and couldn't wait to "Tie the knot."

Remember when you thanked God for getting you through the Silly-Airheads, Gold-Diggers, and Cheaters? Do you remember how thankful you were you found the Queen that won your heart? Being the woman that she is, she was equally ready to jump the broom and get "hitched." Your heart rested securely in hers, and you were so glad to be in love.

That was then, what about now?

One of the common fears that men have is that their future wife will change and begin to remind them of everything they didn't want in a wife and woman. It has been said, "If you want to know what your wife will look like in the future, just look at her mother or the aunt she the most alike." As you know, in the beginning, there is nothing like the new romance and realizing this person loves you deeply. Remember when you hardly ever argued and made sure you saved the last piece of cake or chicken for her? Those days were something else.

Now, it may be hard to spark romance unless you have a date night or a special occasion to celebrate. A birthday means you give a card, flowers, and a small gift or two. An anniversary brings dinner, flowers, and a small gift or two. It seems like the only thing she has to look forward to is, "Dinner, flowers, and maybe a small gift or two." She knows how you shop or have problems with shopping for her. She knows the food you like, and you know her likes. This kind of romance is predictable. It has no life, no creativity. It is just an attempt, and not the romance desired. It's good that you try but ask yourself if she is really happy with the romance you give. Also, ask if you are happy with the romance, she gives you. I'm sure you can think of a few things you would like to change in more than one area of romance. How many things can you think of? How many things would you like to change?

You are the perfect person to finish this book's title, "I Love My Wife, **but...**"

I know, you could tell everyone you met, the story of how much you love her, and in the same breath run down a laundry list of things you would like to change. The funny thing is, she is more than likely saying and feeling the same about you. "I Love My Husband, **but**..."

Who changed?

You both have. You can't point a finger and say, "She is the one that changed on me!" You both have changed because you both have grown. If you have even a small amount of intelligence and are smart enough to take note of things around you, you will learn and grow. That means automatic change. No one grows and remains the same. Like the song says, "Everything Must Change." It's normal, natural, and the way God intended it to be.

Rather than trying to track her changes, ask yourself, and important question. "Do I know myself?" The person that intimately knows himself is ready to get to know others intimately. I have found this to be true. When it comes to dating, we know more about what we want than we know ourselves. We know our address, our high school, and we can recognize our immediate family members. But many have not taken the time to dig into the deep depths of their own heart, mind, and soul. It is sad but true. Most only deal with deep emotions when it comes to hurt, pain, and disappointment. It is only in those times that we stop everything we are doing and begin to think about the emotional turmoil that is going on within. The other time this pause happens is when we are deep in love and are mesmerized by feelings, romance, and dreams of the future. Mainly, our true self and personality is seen the most in traumatic moments.

The danger is that in dating, we are attempting to find a mate. But many times, we do not realize who we are bringing to the table. We are only focused on who we want to come to the table and to be there for us. We may think we're okay, or we may believe we are a good catch, but deep within, we are simply hoping that someone will find value in us and love us.

I'm sure you know what you like. But I must ask, do you really know who you are? How much time have you given to understanding yourself?

You Have a Chance

The best thing you could do or the greatest project you could ever take on is that of self-discovery. This saves you from having many arguments and fights. Why because knowing yourself gives you a foundation to see where she fits and who she truly is to you. The first step to making things better for both of you, is to uncover who you are as a man mentally, emotionally, financially, sexually, and in all other ways that apply.

I'm not saying you are, but you shouldn't have to walk around your wife as if you are walking on eggshells or afraid to speak your mind and heart. You should never feel as if you have to down-play what you think and feel just to make her happy while you suffer. At the same time, knowing yourself will give you insight into what you think, feel, and like, without feeling like you have to apologize for feeling what you feel.

Be a man and own your thoughts and emotions. Then, develop the courage to speak it out loud. I've never heard a woman ask for a weak man. Strong is always the preference. The point here is for you to know yourself and own the person staring at you in the mirror. If you don't respect yourself, how can you expect her to respect you?

> *"You can't lead where you're not willing to go."*

This is only the beginning. You are about to take a journey that will take you deep into the mind and heart of your mate and yourself. You need this. Understanding her better will help you; however, understanding yourself will help you more. We have to start with you because you can't lead someone where you've never been. You have to earn the right to stand as the God-ordained leader of your home and relationship. You are the standard-bearer, the one who establishes what will and will not be allowed to touch your relationship and family. You are important.

When we are finished, you will have a tool to not only better understand your wife, your daughters, your nieces, but also be able to help them to be stronger, better, and more effective.

The added bonus is this also goes for you. You will be better, more in tune, and empowered.

Chapter 2
Purpose Over Problems

> "Who we marry is one of the most important decisions in life. One that will influence the level of happiness, growth, and success, like no other choice."
> **-Nathan Workman**

I know we should never stereotype but, men are usually quieter than women, especially when it comes to emotions, feelings, and intimacy. How many times has your wife or woman asked you, "What are you thinking?" As men, we don't want to go there, particularly if we have a bad thought. Many times, in relationships and marriages, couples don't communicate as they would like or as sincerely and honestly as they need to. Sparing a few hurt feelings for the moment, they set the stage for hurting and disappointing each other later. Often, putting off the hard conversation or the difficult issues only increases the hurt and destruction it will inevitably cause later - now is better. Living in pain, one mate may seek comfort elsewhere, in a hobby, friends, a bottle, or another person's arms. As time moves on, and as the pain continues to grow, you realize that walking around each other as if walking on eggshells is no way to live. It doesn't work.

What do you do about the things you don't like? Really, how do you respond when you see things you don't like that have nothing to do with your marriage or relationship? Let's be real; you see something you can't stand in your wife and wonder what to do about them. You have given it another chance or try to be understanding. You found out that not saying anything about it only makes you more uncomfortable, angry, and sometimes frustrated. In a state of mind like that, you may give up all hope. You may have even said, "I wish I had married KaSandrala (an old girlfriend)!" or "I made a mistake; I wish I could rewind the hands of time." Anyone can do it, but being a man, you may develop a roaming eye or become vulnerable to another woman that will meet the needs, fantasies, and adventures you think your wife isn't.

I have counseled many married couples that all have at least one regret or two. Many of them would make a different choice if they could go back and do it all over. But here is the good news, there is hope for your present and future marriage, even with this person's faults staring at you.

This book aims to help the married, newly married, and even the recently divorced. This book is a tool that will help you to understand the person you married or left, the person they are now, and the person you have become in spite, or because of them.

This book will help you look deeper, beyond the pleasure or pain of your relationship, and understand your relationship's PURPOSE. So far, you have become aware of what you like and don't like, want, and don't want.

What do you want and what do you need?

What you need to do is stop fantasizing, and not waste years of your life by throwing away the marriage/relationship you have. I think it's funny how we, as men, will easily fall into the trap of going after a woman who only fulfills 20% of our "true" needs while rejecting others who met 80% of your needs. I have found that the 20 percent are usually good looking, physically attractive with a body to match, that don't or won't cook, and expect you to treat them like you are a sugar daddy, and are high maintenance. Eye-candy and trophy wives are all for show. You show up with them, instead of growing with them. If you have a woman, you can grow with, stay with her. You also need to understand the opportunity that is right before you.

You have the opportunity to grow, and to understand the necessary changes that must take place in your life. You are here to grow, not to go happily through life without any problems or circumstances or challenges. Realize that there are thousands of people who never get to experience the blessings that you now have. Many men, just like you, wish that they had a woman to love, and a relationship that lasts more than two weeks. Face it; you are blessed. Some men would love to have the woman you have. Even as imperfect as you may think she is.

YOU MUST seek to understand and not undermine the gift that God has given you, in the woman that he has given you. I know that when she does things that you don't like, they rub you the wrong way. Let me remind you, that as she rubs you the wrong way, she is either polishing you or sharpening you. Do not throw away this divine opportunity to become better.

Should I Try To Change Her?

"THE MAN IS THE HEAD!" You heard that before didn't you. You may have even said it yourself. To some men, this means, "She has to do what I say and provide what I like!" Some also think, "She is here to please me!" It doesn't work that way. I have seen this in both men and women. A desire to shape and mold a person into the image you want is dangerous and disrespectful. I understand the problem, and I've heard it all, "No one is perfect, and if I can just 'Help her out in this area…' The problem is, you have to know when and where to help yourself before trying to help her. Remember, you can't lead where you've never been. If you want more honesty and understanding from her, are you more understanding and honest? If you want her to be there for you and believe in you, do you believe in her? Before things get better, you must get better, and before she makes changes, you must make changes. Remember, helping a person to become better in an area they are trying to improve completely different from manipulating, intimidating, or even lovingly insisting they change and conform to your desires. The kind of change often needed, comes through growth and not force or intimidation.

You are not her father, so stop trying to command her as if you are a general in an army. A man with real power never has to force anyone to comply or follow him. She is not a slave to be rewarded with your love and acceptance or even a few dollars when she pleases you. If you treat her that way, you are forcing your wife into a form of prostitution. She has to perform for you to get a dress, nails, or a new hairdo. She doesn't need a pimp; she needs a dedicated partner and unconditional love. Be her husband, not her father, taskmaster, or pimp. Love her as an equal, instead of secretly belittling her or intimidating her with outbursts of anger. If she was wonderful enough to win your heart and marry, she is wonderful enough to keep. There is a hidden treasure in your woman's personality, just as there is in yours.

Even though both of you have changed a little, this book is the key you need to unlock the heart of the woman you now have. It is also the key to unlocking some of the blessings and promises God has for you regarding your marriage, family, and future.

Take this book, begin to understand the gift given to you, and the beautiful future laid before you. But please be warned, as you continue to read, you will face a challenge to grow and change.

If you want to live out the rest of your years in happiness, growth, and divine purpose, keep reading. If you are satisfied with being dissatisfied, and only living to complain about what you don't like, then read no further. I don't want to waste your time.

If you do want to read further, keep in mind this book has a companion, and your wife can take this journey with you. Take the time to read, study, and observe as you consider the words and exercises that this book will take you through. I will use my many years of counseling and ministering to help you and your mate discover the deepest depths of what God originally intended for your marriage.

Now, get ready to grow and become more in love than you ever have been.

Take A Moment

1) Do you feel you know all there is to know about your wife?
2) Are you secretly bored with your wife?
3) When was the last time your wife thrilled you or did something to make you think of her all day long?
4) After you have spent some time observing your wife, complete the following sentence – "I would

love to change the following things about my wife..."
5) I would love to change the following things about my wife. (list at least three, you know you have them)
6) Name five of your wife's favorite things.
7) When was the last time you made sure she had any of those five things consistently?

Hidden Problems in Plain Sight

If I were working with you through those questions, I could look at your answers and tell you where there are hidden problems in plain sight. There is always something more to learn about your wife, as the years pass each of you grow, and you never stop learning about her. If you are secretly bored with your wife, this indicates that you've not only stopped learning about her, but you are probably finding yourself completing question number four: "I think my wife would experience more out of life if she would just..."

Does your wife know what it takes to thrill you? She can't do something she doesn't know how to do or what it takes to do it; I'm wondering, even if it makes you step outside of your comfort zone, will you tell her what it takes to thrill you? Problems become magnified when either mate continually thinks of how to change the other one. The last thing I'll address in the questions posed above is, do you know her favorite things? If you knew them, that's great. If you didn't – start, there. For those that knew them, how intentional are you in making sure she has them? Maybe it's impossible to give her all five all the time, but I'm sure there is a way to provide her with at least one. Finally, relax – remember there's a book for her too.

Chapter 3

Two Personalities One Marriage

"...To start the flow of oxygen, pull the mask towards you. Place it firmly over your nose and mouth, secure the elastic band behind your head, and breathe normally. Although the bag does not inflate, oxygen is flowing to the mask. If you are traveling with a child or someone who requires assistance, secure your mask on first, and then assist the other person."
- **Typical Airline Announcement**

I used to think this was selfish. The first time I heard it, I thought the flight attendants were mistaken in what they had said. Then I thought to myself, why do millions of people hear the above quotation repeated over and over again? You may have flown many times before, but you will still hear this same statement repeated. If you don't know it, let me introduce you to the announcement and the wisdom that is behind it. I was amazed that in this statement, the boards of directors, lawyers, supervisors, and upper management, had all agreed that this statement was correct and necessary. Because it was never known ahead of time if certain pressures would increase to the point of danger, they devised a system that automatically made oxygen masks available. In this dangerous situation, they gave the instruction they thought was important for the wellbeing of everyone. It even states, if you had a child or were sitting next to a person who needed assistance, you would place the mask over your face first, and then upon your child or the person needing help next to you.

What always amazed me about this statement was that the person's child comes after the person's safety and care. It always seemed a little backward to me because I learned to consider others first. And being taught to put others first, it is not difficult to imagine that you would take care of them before considering yourself even in a needy situation. However, true that maybe, these are not the instructions given. The insight that I get from this statement is simple; you have to consider yourself first..

> *"It is best to be selfish when it comes to correcting or bettering yourself, and selfless when it comes to helping, praising, or complementing others."*
> *– unknown*

Here it is again; you have to get help first. I think it is wise to help yourself first, or change first, or pursue wisdom first. Whatever it is, I think it makes sense for you to take the first positive step. Taking care of yourself first means that you are in a better position to help others. Without receiving the help, you need, it becomes more difficult, if not impossible, to help others. A poor man can assist only a few, but a rich man can support many. The other side is that hurt people will always hurt people. Meaning you need the focus and attention first, and then you will be able to see how to help others. Without focusing on yourself first, you run the risk of being self-righteous, uncorrectable, and quick to make your wife or significant other think they are the problem.

I don't know your history or background. I don't know if you have a habit of blaming others or not. However, I know it's time to take responsibility for your actions, and where you are in life and relationships. If we do not focus on ourselves first, we will develop a habit of always pointing the finger at someone else. Doesn't that sound familiar? Arguments continue because one or the other person continues to point the finger at the other person. The way to defuse an argument is to point the finger at yourself. This works for any corrective measure that needs to be taken of, whether it is a challenging argument, conversation, or misunderstanding.

You Married A Person

To put that in other words, you married a personality. You married someone with a personality type that has been on this earth for millions of years. You married someone that has a pattern to the way they think, act, speak, and react. The same goes for you. You have a habit of acting, thinking, and behaving the way you do. Because its best to start where you are, we begin with you and your personality.

For this book's purpose, you will need to focus on yourself before attempting to help or diagnose the other person in your life. Meaning before you can begin to unravel your partner's personality, you will need to dig into your own personality, habits, and mindset before attempting to understand and correct the same in your partner. Let's make sure that you have the oxygen you need, before attempting to put the mask on your mate. In this case, we want to take off all the masks that we can before helping others to see more clearly.

Your Personality And The Elements

Not to stereotype but, men don't usually think this deeply about personality or even psychological matters. Most men would rather watch a game than try to understand the game they are playing on themselves. But, how many times have you seriously thought about yourself as a person? Or let me ask this question. When was the last time you thought about your psychological makeup or asked yourself why you thought, felt, or acted a certain way, and sincerely answered?

These two questions may seem a little strange to you, if so, then you have something in common with everyone. As the man, you are probably playing the role of provider, counselor, Mr. Fixit, and many other things. You are busy just like the rest of us. That's why we often do not look at ourselves because we are too busy looking at the other person, - pointing the finger. Many of us are eagerly looking at other people's faults and problems while being as blind as a bat to our own faults and problems. It's true for everyone but especially true for those who are in a relationship. Maybe it's because we spend more time with ourselves than anyone else, and think that we know ourselves. The problem is, we do not know ourselves as deeply as we believe. Many of us are strangers to ourselves. Some of the things we know are how we look when we get hungry and what we need on a fundamental level. But, when it comes to who we really are, many of us do not have a clue about ourselves. But that does not stop us from trying to correct others, or read other people's mail, or even tell them a thing or two. Even amid a heated conversation, we are so sure that we are right.

Being a man, I can say this about us. We feel as if we have to know more than those in our household. We have to know best, even if we don't know more, because we learn to play the head's role instead of being the head. We saw from our fathers, television characters, and even relatives that the man must dominate. We are the head of the household. The problem men face is when you think you know and don't; it makes you look terrible to those that do. Let's face it; your wife knows more about certain things than you do. Pride will bring you to your knees. You look a lot better when you are honest and say something like, "I don't know, but let me find out…"

Every person I have counseled, every person I have helped, helped because they were open to correction, and open to understanding more about the situation than they did before. This is where you must be in a position to understand more about you, your relationship, and the future of your marriage. It's the wrong time to think you have everything figured out, and you do not need any further information. Your marriage or relationship is where it is because of your level of thinking and understanding. I know it is not you alone, you're in this together.

You are not any less of a man because you don't have all the answers. You are more of a man when your family can depend on whatever you say as being the truth. Your ability to think deeper and understand more than you have before will be the key to unlocking new doors and new avenues for your relationship to grow. Also, by being open-minded, you can learn more and achieve the goals that you desire in your marriage.

The First challenge in opening your mind is in the area of your personality. I have heard it said that the way to get through a difficult subject is by making it easy to understand. Like telling a story, or a joke, we know it and, therefore, can quickly get the punchline. Sometimes making the point by trying to sound philosophical or scientific, doesn't get the job done. In fact, it makes things worse. This is why I have chosen to make the difficult and complex subject of your personality as easy and comfortable as possible to understand. The first challenge involves you, understanding your pattern. Each of us operate and react to a pattern. It is as much a part of us as anything else. This pattern controls how we react to pressure or seek joy and affirmation. This pattern also helps us understand what is and isn't valuable to us. One person's pattern maybe they get easily angered and upset; another person's maybe sitting quietly and never saying a word unless literally on fire. You know the kind of person I'm talking about! You either know one or are one. There is also another pattern or two that covers the type of person that is bold and outspoken. This person doesn't wait till he is on fire to speak; he sets others on fire. And then there is the person that makes things serious and easily shows you every reason why the glass is half empty.

Breaking Down the Elements

The foundation of exploring the elements of your personality is knowing and understanding your pattern. It is as much a part of us as anything else. This pattern programs us as to how we react to stress or seek joy and affirmation. It also helps us understand what is and isn't important to us. One person's pattern may be that they are easily excited and talkative; another person may be sitting quietly and never saying a word unless literally on fire. You either know one or are one. There is also another pattern or two that covers the kind of person that is bold and outspoken.

This person doesn't wait until he is on fire to speak; he sets others on fire. Then, there is the person who takes things seriously and quickly shows you every reason why the glass is half empty.

The way I describe our specific patterns is by looking at the elements. We have the four basic elements, and without them, we can't live: earth, air, fire, and water. In understanding your wife and removing the but I am sharing excerpts from my book Mastering Your Personality. This book goes even deeper into the highlights I am sharing with you now. Understanding personalities go back centuries, literally. A physician named Claudius Galenus was a leader in developing the personality terms Melancholy, Sanguine, Choleric, and Phlegmatic. If you are familiar with the D.I.S.C. system developed by psychologist William Moulton Marston, you may know these terms as Dominance, Influence, Steadiness, and Conscientious. I am choosing to provide both references to guide you through understanding yourself and your mate.

Earth (Melancholy, C)

The Earth Personality is an introverted, logical, analytical, factual, private, 'let's-do-it-right" person. Earth Personalities respond to others in a slow, cautious, and indirect manner. Earth Personalities are reserved and suspicious until sure of your intentions.

The Earth Personality, probes for the "hidden meaning" behind your words. They are timid and may appear unsure and have a serious expression. They are self-sacrificing, gifted, and they tend to be a perfectionist. Earth Personalities are very sensitive to what others think about their work. The Earth Personality is well organized; on occasion, you may find an Earth Personality that keeps things cluttered; however, they know what's in the piles. The Earth Personality is determined to make the right and best decision. Earth Personalities will ask specific questions, and sometimes they will ask the same question again and again.

Air (Sanguine, I)

Air is refreshing, light, and indispensable. What would an air personality be like? Air is everything mentioned and more, including unstable. Continue to read and see if you are an Air personality.

The Air Personality is an extroverted, fun-loving, activity-prone, impulsive, entertaining, persuasive, easily amused, and optimistic person. Air Personalities are receptive and open to others and build relationships quickly. They are animated, excited, and accepting of others. They will smile and talk easily and often. It is not unusual to feel as if you have known the Air Personality for years after only a few minutes.

Fire (Choleric, D)

We have all come in contact with fire, and also Fire Personalities.

The Fire Personality is an extroverted, hot-tempered, quick-thinking, active, practical, strong-willed, and easily annoyed person. Fire Personalities are self-confident, self-sufficient, and very independent-minded. They are decisive and opinionated and find it easy to make decisions for themselves as well as others.

Water (Phlegmatic, S)

The Water Personality is an introverted, calm, unemotional, easygoing, never-get-upset, person. Water Personalities are both slow and indirect when responding to others. They are also reluctant to warm-up but will be accommodating in the process. Water Personalities are by far the easiest person with which to get along. They live a quiet, routine life free of the other temperaments' normal anxieties and stresses. The Water Personality will avoid getting too involved with people and life in general. Water Personalities seldom exert themselves with others or push their way along in their career; they just let it happen.

Defining Your Element

Did you find yourself? As you read, were you thinking, "Yes, that sounds like me, or No, it doesn't!" We are quick to own the good things about ourselves and pretend like the bad doesn't exist. I must say, there is something about knowing the truth and recognizing a cold hard fact about yourself that is undeniable. You know you hit the nail on the head and can acknowledge a part of you within the descriptions. I'm sure you have noticed a number of the attributes and character traits from the above descriptions. The question is, "Which are you willing to own?"

I have to warn you. To get your attention, I will have to say some of the things I mention with a little extra boldness. I may even say a few things for shock value. There is enough truth in the listed character traits to recognize yourself. Is it a perfect description? No, a perfect description is not what is needed here. The purpose is not to nail your personality to the wall just yet. It's like the coach told his team-mate who was anxious to hit a home-run. After seeing the player use up just about all of his energy with imaginary swings in the locker room, he told him, "You have to get in the ballpark first before you can hit a home-run." I am merely trying to get you in the ballpark first.

Try This

Take out a sheet of paper or choose one in a notebook. Write down the four basic styles, "Earth, Air,

Fire, and Water." Out of the general descriptions given, number, and name the traits that you see in yourself. Don't be surprised that you have a few others or a little of all of them.

Review your findings and notice the most significant number of items listed under each heading. If there are more of one than the other, you will know where the "Ball-Park" is. If you have an equal number in two headings like "Fire" or "Water," don't be surprised.

Here is how you handle your fork in the road:

Sit back and relax. Think of how you are or how you would like to be "Most of the Time." Here is where you will have to go with your gut feeling and allow your inner compass to guide and steer you correctly. How do you feel about being a (blank) or a (blank)? Ask yourself and allow your heart to settle on the right choice for you peacefully.

You will see later that there are secondary personality traits, as well as the primary type. For now, let's get you in the ballpark so that we can take you further into your journey of self- discovery.

I know what you are thinking, "I thought this was about my Wife or Significant Other?" It is, but remember, we have to get you the help you need before you attempt to help them.

*Now that you have a hint of your Element and Personality Type, find and review the full description of your major personality type from the full descriptions above.

Take this opportunity to get to know yourself a little better.

> *A good wife is one who serves her husband in the morning like a mother does, loves him in the day like a sister does and pleases him like a prostitute in the night.* - **Chanakya**

Here is a quick little test to see if you are happy or not. If you see a young couple and think to yourself, "They don't know what they are in for, just wait till they wake up!" If you have thought this, then yes, you need a little help. Have you heard it said, "You are just in the honeymoon stage, just wait?" Or maybe you heard, "You two love each other, hope it lasts." Many well-wishers secretly desire your marriage to end up like theirs, miserable. I think misery does love company, but it doesn't have to be you keeping it company.

You love your wife for a good reason, and you want to make things better, which is why you are reading my book. By understanding the personality types of Earth, Air, Fire, and Water, you saw not only yourself but also your wife. Without getting into stereotypes, I won't say that men are slower to see emotional and spiritual truths than women are. I'm not going to say that. I will say that a man attentive to his wife's personality and make-up is more equipped to lead and love her. The days of putting your foot down and expecting her to obey blindly are over. Today's woman must know that you have her best interest at heart and that you will love, protect, and provide for her. The man who chooses to understand a woman's heart and soul is already halfway to winning her heart forever. Some say women are wiser and more perceptive than men. I'm not going to touch that but, I will say that women can indeed be perceptive if they choose to be. After looking at the personality types, you saw some things and may have even smiled at how you noticed bits and pieces of your wife's personality.

Let's take a look at the different personality types again, but this time, let's look at the positive and remember why you love your wife. No matter where you are in your marital relationship, it's always good to remind yourself why you love her as you do.

If your wife is an Earth Personality:

You may love her thoroughness. You trust and feel secure in her ability to make decisions and also like that she takes her time. She isn't persuaded by the hype or excitement of others but does what she feels is right. You feel secure knowing that she is digging into the subject will make her opinion, wisdom, and suggestion; the best way to go. The result will be as solid and secure as she is. You also may feel her ability to "Keep it real" is refreshing, especially after dealing with deceivers in your past.

If your wife is an Air Personality:

You may love the life she brings to the everyday grind. She is the life of the party, takes care of her appearance, and is engaging. You may love her ability to be spontaneous and carefree. You may love the friendship and ability to discuss things when you want to get something off your chest or express yourself. Sometimes, there are just things you need to say. It's good when she has a listening ear and a listening heart, waiting for you just to speak.

If your wife is a Fire Personality:

One of the things you may love about her is her intense "drive." You love the fact that she has plans and makes things happen. You wanted a woman that had a vision, and you have one in your Fire Personality wife. You love that when she sets her mind to something, she gets it done. You have the confidence in her that someway, somehow, she will come through for you. You also love how she doesn't give up, even when things look their worst.

If your wife is a Water Personality:

It's easy to see why you would love so many of her qualities. You may love her easy flowing, easy-going way of dealing with things. It takes her a while to get upset or lose her temper. You may also admire her ability to feel and empathize with you. You think that she is considerate and conscious of your feelings, wishes, and desires.

Take a moment to write down and review the many things you love about your wife. I am asking you to write and consider what you love about your wife. This list will be very valuable in times of storm when the sailing doesn't seem to be going as smoothly as you want. It is always a good time to remember the good in her.

You fell in love with your wife for all the reasons you've written down. As you write and review, you see the very reason you had a honeymoon season, to begin with. When you review, understand that you now hold the key to creating the honeymoon atmosphere whenever you wish.

Take notice. Even as you began reviewing, reminiscing, and smiling, your feelings changed. Notice that whatever you have been going through, you feel better about your relationship because you remembered what you love about your wife.

Let me ask a good question that helps with the next section. When the honeymoon season ended, where did it go? What part of your wife are you experiencing during the bad times? Isn't she the same woman you fell in love with?

- We are two opposites that attract and find ourselves opposite on almost everything but stay together anyway.
- We are two opposites that attract and have found a harmony that helps us build each other up and provide what the other doesn't have.
- We are so compatible, it's crazy. We have more years under our belt than we've had arguments - We never fight.
- We are so much alike that we fight all the time. Most days I love her, other days, I wonder who's sleeping in my bed.
- Our relationship is complicated in that we understand what we don't like about the other person and are okay with it - it's our cross to bear.
- God has given us to each other, and I just want to be better for her.
- I want to give her what she needs.

Understanding Your Needs

As the head of the household, let's make sure we're on the same page. Let's review you.

We all have needs, right? Just like you may feel as if your needs aren't being met when you nudge her in the night, she says she has a headache; she has emotional, even psychological needs. You also have the same emotional and psychological needs. Face it, no matter what your element or type is, your personality has needs. When you don't receive what your personality type needs, you feel less than happy. You don't like it and begin to feel frustrated as you continue to try to deal with everyday life.

If you can't breathe, after two minutes, things become dangerous. You could die. When the body goes without water for five days, death becomes possible. Even though your emotional, psychological, and spiritual endurance allows you more time, it's only a matter of time before you begin to die. I don't want you to be like others who have been neglected emotionally and spiritually so that now they exist in a dead relationship. This is why many have Zombie relationships - they are walking dead relationships filled with neglect, pain, and dysfunction. Death on this level comes slowly and little at a time. It's an interesting thing, but getting just a little bit of what you need helps but may do more bad than good.

Do you have a Zombie relationship - a relationship that is dead, but it keeps on walking? Let me explain what this means to you, your relationships, and your inner health. Not getting what your personality needs makes you feel unappreciated, disconnected, and puts you in survival mode. After a long while, you become used to not getting what you want. You become accustomed to living and loving in pain. Then, out of nowhere, you get a little crumb of what you need. Like a sip of water to the thirsty, you feel great and remember how good things could be. The danger is, going back into another long season of not getting what you want, you can begin to lose hope. The thoughts start to flood your mind that the little crumb you keep getting after a long time isn't enough. As you continue to lose hope, you begin to fight the temptation to seek comfort in the woman on the job that told you she would be there for you. Rather than the little you receive showing you that there is hope, it becomes something else. Thoughts may enter your mind like, "See, she could give me what I need, but she doesn't care. She must not want me, or she must have someone else…"

You shouldn't be the only one to know what you need. Let's take a look at the types and see what you need.

If you are an Earth Personality

If you are an Earth Personality, you need patience and understanding. You don't need to be reminded of why you take longer than others to make up your mind. You need understanding and the freedom to go with what you think is best. As your wife begins to understand your need for information and the time to process things, you will feel free to do what you need to. You need patience, the time to process, and think things through as many times as you need to. It must be understood that you are merely trying to make the right decision and do the right thing.

You also need encouragement and affirmation. Because you may be tempted to see the glass as half-full, you need regular installments of affirmation, positivity, and patience. There are more needs, but these take you a long way down the road.

If you are an Air Personality
You need variety, engagement, and creativity. You desire to enjoy while being productive. You have a need to discover, create, and communicate. Like Air, you need room to flow, and someone to help you stay on task. As mentioned above, there is more to your needs, but these are your major areas of concern.

If you are a Fire Personality
You need an inspiring atmosphere, a cause, or a challenge, and you need a helping hand. You have a lot on your plate because you keep it that way. Some may ask the question if you need stress to function. You simply need to feel the inspiration and vitality necessary to get and keep you moving. You need someone to be as aware and excited about your vision as you are. There's more to your needs, but with these being covered, the rest will follow.

If you are a Water Personality
You need an atmosphere of consistency, dependability, and solid leadership. You need a tactful and honest

leader to communicate the direction you need to go while allowing you to voice your needs and feelings. You also need an atmosphere that is as stress-free as possible. Because you love and relate to others with honesty and integrity, you need others to have the same integrity and conviction that you do. Without it, it's difficult for you to trust.

Take A Moment

Now that you know your personality areas of need that you agree with from the descriptions above. Be sure to write down any needs that were not mentioned, as you will use them to share with your wife. Don't leave anything out. All of it is necessary. You may notice your list of "needs" is longer; there can be many reasons for that. One point of consideration is that you have a secondary personality, and that changes things a little.

Have you considered your wife's secondary personality? Do you think there are other needs not listed that she may have? What about considering if her needs have changed since you married? In the next section, I want you to look at how, why, and where you've seen changes.

1) Do you feel you receive most of the encouragement and affirmation you need from others or from your wife?
2) Imagine you are at home alone, and you can breathe deeply, relax, and be yourself. Are you

able to easily feel the same way when you are around your wife?

3) When was the last time you felt like having fun or perhaps have been drawn in by an attractive stare? Was your wife included in this moment?

4) Are you still attracted to your wife?

5) How easy would it be for another woman to steal you away from your wife?
    a. What would she have to say or do?
    b. How would she have to look?
    c. What did you feel while responding to this question?
    d. Have you considered your level of commitment to your marriage or relationship?

Chapter 4
Honesty Heals

> Positive feelings come from being honest about yourself and accepting your personality, and physical characteristics, warts and all; and, from belonging to a family that accepts you without question.
> **- Willard Scott**

If you were like me, I hesitated before I married because I was always wondering if I should hold out for "Better." I knew that there was better out there, but who doesn't like "Better?" Better even sounds better.

A comedian once told a story in the form of a joke.

There was a Mall where women could literally shop for a husband. Like many department stores, it had levels. As you can guess, the higher levels had better selections of men than the lower levels. A particular woman walked and was introduced to the men on the first level. Looking around, she easily noticed all the pot-bellied men who wore stained shirts, some with bigger holes than others. Personal hygiene was optional, but each of them smiled and welcomed the opportunity. The elevator arrived, and she went to the next level. There the men were clean-shaven, a little lighter on their feet, but none of them worked or had their own teeth. Dissatisfied and going through the next number of levels, this woman arrived on the last two floors. The men were fit and muscular; they were kind and cordial and even had their own teeth. The only thing standing taller than their average 6 foot 2 height was the stacks of hundreds they had. Each of them earned over six figures, honestly loved and respected the women in their lives, and earned over two-hundred thousand a year. She thought she died and went to heaven. But she thought and thought. "If this is the next to last level, what kind of men are on the next level?" She was informed the last level was a "Special" level that needed an attendant to accompany her. Finding an attendant, she got on the elevator and couldn't wait to see what she would find on this level. "Ding!" the elevator opened its doors, and she noticed the floor was full of women. Confused, she asked the attendant about the men on the floor and wondered why there were so many women. The attendant informed her, "This is the special floor designated for women who are never satisfied with a good man."

This joke told by a comedian is true for many people, both male and female alike.

What Is Better?

Out of the many volumes of books written and audio recordings gathered, the total of the male-female relationship is said to be that, "Men are from Mars, Women are from Venus." This represents a vast difference between the two. Yes, there are men closer to Venus and women closer to Mars, but there is still a notable difference. One difference is on the definition of "Better." Better is a matter of perception. "Better to some, is worse for others." When it comes to understanding personalities in relationships, "Better" has a lot to do with what is wanted or expected. It goes even beyond personality.

Remember when you were younger? You saw your mother and father's relationship and may have wanted a woman like your mother. If you didn't have a mother, maybe you saw someone on television or perhaps even had a first love that was everything you wanted. When it came time to marry, you could have chosen someone who was "like" all the positive relationships and experiences you had ever known. Add the unique needs and desires of your personality, and you have an interesting mix for what your "Better" would be. I said it before, and I'll say it again, "We don't always know what we want, but we always want what we have known."

How do you know when "Better" has arrived? Everyone is different. What we want and expect is different. Simply put, we perceive better is happening when we are getting what we want. If you grew up as the young man above, you might have seen your mother as the ultimate female example. Expecting your wife to be another version of your mother, you think things are good when you feel she's acting like your mother. When you feel your wife isn't acting like your mother, you may think she is not what you wanted. It also happens the other way around. You may choose someone to be the opposite of your mother, but the same rules apply. When they don't act like your mother, things are good, when they do, things are bad. Play the scenario out any way you want; whether looking for someone like a past love or even your mother, your "Better" could just be a comparison of what you experienced at home or in your single days.

Is Better Good For You?

God created man in His image, and we would love to create women in ours. If we had things our way, we would make things just like we wanted. We would be wealthy, muscular, able to eat a horse, never gain weight, and never grow old. The problem is, eating a horse, defying time, and being idle because of wealth, isn't good for you. Challenge, change, adversity, and hard situations are good for you. It is a fact that when you get what you want all the time, it ruins you.

Let me let you in on a secret. Many women feel that most men are just little boys who pout when they don't get their way. Many women who naturally adore their sons, have similar affections for their husbands and their sons, but with important boundaries and filters in place. They would never confuse the two of you, but most women understand that they will have to "Work With" their husbands and "Help" him. It adds to the "Help-Meet" role of the Christian wife and a burden to the un-Christian wife. No woman should have to sleep with someone she has had to help raise.

What's the Problem?

Many men are used to getting what they want from "Momma." Most girls are used to getting what they want from "Daddy." Setting up a hidden program within the mind saying, "My wife must give me whatever I want." This also works for daughters and fathers. It causes your wife to think that you will respond to her as her father did. We will discuss this further later. Let me ask a question.

Have you been ruined or spoiled by getting what you want? If you received everything you ever wanted, when you wanted it, you would become self-centered and begin to think the purpose of everyone, and everything was to get you what you wanted - it's all about you. The first person to feel this the most would be your wife. When something is spoiled, it usually makes others sick. Is your wife sick of you, but not telling you? Is she telling her girlfriend or another man instead?

I hope you know that everyone and everything is not here just to serve you. As an example, there's nothing wrong with breakfast in bed every now and then. As an example, think of receiving breakfast in bed every day. Breakfast in bed would no longer be special; it would just be the way things are.

I said that to say, if your wife always gave you better, better wouldn't be special anymore. You need a little of what "Worse" brings to the table and the "Better.' Let's look at a little of what you need.

Take A Moment

1) Name 3 things your wife didn't do for you that upset you.
2) Name 3 things you didn't do for your wife that upset her.
3) Were these things necessary like bills, picking up the kids, or something extra like fixing a plate for dinner?
4) On a sheet of paper, write out what would be "better" for you in your home and marital relationship. Don't miss anything and take your time. This isn't a race; it's a journey.
5) Look at what you've written for number four and cross out any items you already have.
6) With the items that are left, can you have a discussion with your mate about your "better." Will she be surprised at what you need? Will she become angry?

For Worse

Many men are used to getting what they want from "Momma." Most girls are used to getting what they want from "Daddy." It sets up a hidden program within the mind that says, "My wife must give me whatever I want." This also works for daughters and fathers. It causes your wife to think that you will respond to her as her father did. We will discuss this further later. Let me ask a question.

Have you been ruined or spoiled by getting what you want? If you received everything you ever wanted, when you wanted it, you would become self-centered and begin to think the purpose of everyone, and everything was to get you what you wanted - it's all about you. The first person to feel this the most would be your wife. When something is spoiled, it usually makes others sick. Is your wife sick of you, but not telling you? Is she telling her girlfriend or another man instead?

The last thing you want to hear as a man is that things are getting worse in your marriage or that your best days are behind you. Who wants to hear that worse is coming instead of better? I can't think of anyone that would rather have worse instead of better. Can you?

When you were married, did you think there would be more "good than bad," more "better than worse?" No one expects to suffer when getting married. It's all about the love and commitment and the vows to last a lifetime. I know two people pitching in around the house makes things a lot better. Two people cleaning, cooking, and paying bills is far better than just one person having to do it all. Whether she cooks or cleans, it helps. So, you are right; some things have gotten better.

You can't have your way all the time, and things may be good for a while, but bad or worse is coming. I don't want to depress you or tell you something that will hurt you. That is not my purpose. My purpose is to shed some light on your hard spots and the dark times in your marriage or relationship. You don't need help when things are going well. You need a hand when things get rough, and you feel like throwing in the towel or borrowing someone else's.

Outside Sources

How can I help you see that even in the roughest places in your marriage, there is still good there? I can help you by pointing out a few things you should know. First, there's a part of the better and worse in marriage and relationships from outside sources. These are things from places you didn't expect like, getting a pink slip because the company is downsizing after giving you a raise, one of the kids being sick or getting in an accident, and unexpected bills. I could go on and on, but you get my point. Those things come from the outside to challenge you. They have to be defeated by you and your wife on the inside of your home. Together, you and she handle whatever comes to your door, she may greet hers first, but you handle it together. She needs you, and you need her to handle ALL the situations that challenge you.

This is a good habit to practice. When anything or anyone approaches you from the outside (outside your home or relationship), you both greet it and meet it as one. Whether its old friends, new co-workers, or even family members. This helps to handle some of the "Worse" things that could happen.

Never From The Outside!

The most dangerous threats to your marriage or relationship never come from the outside; they come from the inside. They begin, inside you and inside her, or inside your home. As I show you more and more of your personality with its weaknesses and strengths, you will see where you may bring a challenge to the marriage. For now, let's talk about her.

Both you and she have the power to destroy your marriage. It doesn't take much. I heard years ago, "It takes $5 million to build a bridge, but only $500 of dynamite to blow it up!" Marriage and happiness can be very fragile, even delicate.

The Value of Happiness

You feel happy about your marriage when the top 3 to 5 things you value are being cared for like you want. If you appreciate having a clean house, you are happy when she picks up after herself. If you like having a few dollars in your pocket, you love it when she helps you budget, plan, and contribute. If you want romantic gestures, you are happy when she dresses extra sexy in private and showers you with kisses and hugs. You have a list of things that you want to see, feel, hear, and experience because they are valuable to you. This is why they are called "Values." This also means that they are not the only thing you want, but they are more important than the next fifty things you could name.

When you two got together, you fell in love partly because of what you saw, and mostly because of what you wanted to see. What was important to you was also important to her so, you got along famously as they say. You hit it off and decided to jump the broom and tie the knot. The only problem is, just as you have three to five things that are important to you, she does too. The other fifty things you could name are below the surface. Think of the iceberg that sunk the Titanic. To the naked eye, it didn't appear to be anything. But what inevitably sunk the ship was underneath the surface.

Marriage and relationships are the same way. The things that challenge your marriage are underneath the surface. Over time, the icebergs in your life hiding underneath the surface show up. When they appear, the three to five things that are important to you are no longer at the top of her list. Things have changed.

The problem is not that she fooled you or tricked you. The challenge came because she grew and began to show some of her other personality traits, and what she needed to be more of herself. She is growing just like you. You are not the only one with a new mindset or a new way of thinking. Give her credit. Think about it. If you have an old- wineskin mentality, your marriage will not be able to stretch and grow as each of you grow. As time goes on, you will grow and want to experience new things, do different things than what you did before or in your early days of marriage or romance. That is normal.

If you refuse to let her grow, you will eventually lose her. If you fight her growth, she will grow to resent you. If you try to mold her into the image of your mother or a past lover, you will be sadly disappointed when you realize that you have lost all three, your mother that she could never be, the past lover gone from your life, and the wife you will soon lose if you don't get a grip on yourself.

It is only insecurity and fear that makes you want to control or dominate her. Believing your own lie, you think you know what's best for her because you wear pants and wears a skirt. That's not a good reason. "Because I'm A Man!" That means nothing at all. Father doesn't always know what's best for mamma; he needs to ask mamma and take notes.

Indeed men and women think differently. Most women think a man having a place in her heart gives him a place in her life. Men think winning a woman's heart secures him a place in her bed and sometimes pocketbook. Having a place in her heart means you are a part of her world, which makes it better, without trying to shape her into the image you think is better.

Remember, your better is what you think you want and need, not your real needs. You want and need love and security; you need affirmation and loving arms to encourage your growth and happiness. You don't really want to love and sleep with a version of your mother, do you? You don't really want to sleep with someone you are fathering and scolding all the time, do you? Isn't that a form of incest?

You may have loved seeing your father being treated like a king by your mother and wanted the same. Or you may have seen your father cheat on and beat your mother, and think that is how you love. NO, IT's NOT! You may have looked for images of your mother in every woman you ever dated. You may have loved being cared for as momma's little man. I don't want to take that away from you, but you are not your mamma's little man any more. Don't make your wife your mother, a past love, or anyone else. Let her be herself, and she will appreciate you for it.

Mistaken Identity

Okay, I know you are not saying you wanted to marry your mother. Most boys grow to love their mothers and have a strong connection with them, even though they may not communicate often. As you know, we men can be that way sometimes.

When you look at your mother, you may see the character of a good woman, and that is what you want. You may see a faithful woman, a loving mother, and a house-maker. There is nothing wrong with that. I hope you agree with me. The only thing is, you must never confuse the attributes for the woman that was your mother. Every woman that I have counseled has all of the good traits of a woman. They may have been misplaced or violently disjointed by trauma, hurt,

pain, disappointment, or other traumas, but it's all there. (We will talk about this more, al little later.)
Let's see if you can answer a few questions about how you view your wife's identity.

Take A Moment

1) Does your wife remind you of anyone from your past? If yes, does she remind you of more than one person? Who are they?
2) Is your wife like your mother at all?
3) Do you still hold fond memories in your heart of a past relationship, person, or experience? If yes, have you tried recreating them secretly with your wife? Be honest.
4) Answer truthfully, do you still "hold a torch" for someone in your past?
5) Do you live in regret, secretly wishing you had married someone else?

Secret Desires

Let's talk about question #5 above - "Do you live in regret, secretly wishing you had married someone else?" It can be a challenging question to consider, but it is a necessary question to ask. This is one of those questions that make you ask, "Did he really ask me that?" It is also one of those questions that make you a little uncomfortable to ask, but also just as uncomfortable in hearing what the answer might be. We both have heard, "Don't ask questions you don't want to know the answer to." It's one of those questions you must "Man-up" to answer. So, are you ready, can you be honest with yourself and answering the question?

You should know that the answer to the question is not my main goal. The answer is not the destination; it's only part of the journey. If you are living in regret because you married the wrong person, you will think of this other "dream-person" off and on. It doesn't matter if things are good or bad between you and the wife; this other dream-person will just pop up in your mind.

You should know that whoever this person is, they are just a dream-person. If you spent as much time with them as you have your wife, you could still be thinking about someone else. The truth is, it's not them, it's you. You are the reason you are not satisfied.

As a man, you remember who treated you the best, made the best connection with you, and made you feel the most complete out of all those in the past. You remember, don't you? There are a few who can say that I married the one I'm thinking about, but so many can't. I think you can.

As the man of the house, you need to name or label that particular person only for the sake of identifying them. Since they are a constant memory, you need to recognize the personality traits you saw in them. I really should use the word perceive because you didn't know that person as well as you may think. Remember the iceberg from the previous chapter? There was much more to that person than what you knew at the time. That person (if they exist) was valuable only because they held the key to what unlocked another part of your heart. You perceived that they were a certain way, and you admired their personality.

The attributes you saw in them exist in your wife. She may show it differently, but it's there. Second, there is a part of you that valued and wanted what the other person from your past **represented**. What part of you wants this person to remain in your life? What part of you still thinks about them? Whatever part it is, have you shown that side of yourself to your wife, or have you been hiding this secret from her? I am not asking if you got into an argument about it. Have you sat down and calmly let her know that there is another part of you who wants or needs this?

The last reason for asking you question number five deals with growth. What is it about you that hasn't grown beyond this point of need or desire? In other words, why are you still here dealing with this old baggage?

In answering that question, you have to look at what that interaction was doing for you. What were you getting out of it? A better way to ask is, how did this person make you feel?

Once you answer how they made you feel, you can see the person for what they really were, a key or a bridge to exploring how you want to feel daily. Again, it's not about them; it's about you!

Past Relationships As Keys and Bridges

This person(s) was a key that unlocked other parts of your iceberg hiding under the surface. They were a bridge that took you from the normal everyday living into feeling like you were really alive, or really in love, or really happy. That is the purpose they served, to simply help you see that part of yourself, and not to be the source of that life or love. They were there to show you, not grow with you.

In reality, what they showed you was a hidden strength or desire in your personality. It was only in your hidden desire to be, and grow that you saw the need to hold on to them. Strangely, they were the **key** to you experiencing that part of yourself, the bridge that took you to a new place.

The truth is, you don't need them anymore. You don't need them! You don't need anyone else in your marriage, but you and your wife.

You have to Un-clutter your mind, heart, and bedroom from other people. Get this fantasy out of your head and focus on the one that is in your heart. It's time to give them the right boot of disfellowshipping. The way to get rid of them is to recognize what they helped you see and be, own it for yourself, and then release them from your heart and memory. It's as simple as that. You don't have room for anyone else in your happy home.

If this person was meant to be a permanent part of your life, they would still be with you instead of wherever they are. Release them and let them go; they have served their purpose. It is true; people come into your life either for a "Reason" or a "Season." Stop getting stuck on the season and embrace the reason.

They were a simple tool to help you see and know your **Personality's Strengths.**

Take A Moment

1) Out of all the past relationships you've had, which one is the most memorable?
2) What made that relationship more memorable than the others? Was it pain, pleasure, or a combination of both?
3) List the things that are memorable and what you feel you got out of the relationship?
4) What would it take for your wife to get the same response out of you that relationship got out of you?
5) If your most memorable relationship was negative, how glad are you that your present relationship doesn't give you the same problem?
6) How and when do you plan to celebrate this and let your wife know you appreciate her love and care?

Chapter 5
Complex Issues With Simple Solutions

"Always be yourself, express yourself, have faith in yourself, do not go out and look for a successful personality and duplicate it."
- **Bruce Lee**

I'm going to introduce a few subject matters that often cause complex issues in marriages. It's necessary to address key areas because if you don't, there will always be a **but** in your marriage. Let's talk about finances, communication, stress, and sex. For the person tempted to put the book down (or throw it across the wall), and for the one asking, are you serious? Yes, and for a good reason.

I'm going to give you insight on who she could be if you helped her make the changes she wants. For instance, if you have a Fire wife and you see that she isn't leading or taking charge, then you know she is feeling frustrated, and something is wrong, she needs you. It gives you a chance to compare the way she is acting, with her potential.

At the end of each section, you will find a strategy for dealing with your wife as it relates to Finances, Communication, Stress, and Sex and Intimacy. I give you tips and hints on how to bring out the best in her in all these areas.

As a man and leader, it's impossible for you to lead someone to where you haven't been before. That means this is a chance for you to do some work on yourself. Yes, you need to work on you. You may think she is the problem. Every problem has a lock that keeps it from dying and one that unlocks it. The truth is, you are both the lock and key to many of her problems. Remember, this is also a chance for you to take inventory of yourself. Compare how your personality fits with hers in these areas. As you look at yourself, think of the strategies as ways that you can make changes.

Suppose you have not identified your personality type and your wife's personality type, as discussed in Chapter 3 – Two Personalities, One Marriage – pause right here and go back and do this. In that case, it is necessary to move forward.

Take A Moment

Think of how you feel and what you need, and describe the kind of mate that would make you happy in the four areas we are discussing. This has nothing to do with your mate; this is simply the wish list you'd write if it were perfect. Don't go crazy, but please be honest and realistic.

Finish the following thoughts:

1) Considering my finances, in a perfect world, my mate would...
2) Considering communication, in a perfect world, my mate would...
3) Considering stress, in a perfect world, my mate would...
4) Considering sex, in a perfect world, my mate would...

Consider Your Strengths

Many of us don't have a problem recognizing and feeling our strengths as men. Life happens to all of us and gives all of us high stress, comfort, crisis, and even a need to talk things out. In those times, a part of you wakes up. Suppose you see that some things get under your skin or make you glad. That is why I want to take this time to highlight the strengths of your personality. You should know your strengths. Learning a secret from those successful in business, "You market on your strengths, and hire on your weakness." As husband and leader, you lead with your strengths and learn from your weaknesses.

To show you your strengths will help you to see the strengths of your wife. I also want to show you that the things you admired in past lovers also belong to your wife. In highlighting your strengths, I want to show you how the same power and strength can be found in each of the major personality types.

Make sure you know your major personality type. (Forget about your wife's for now.) As you read this chapter, keep in mind that we discuss the romantic and marital side of personality types and their strengths. Remember, first, you find yourself, work on yourself, then you find your wife and try to understand more about her - not change her.

In this part of the book, we will see how each personality type views love with their own "Love Language" hints. Keep in mind, people are different, but there is a basic pattern to everyone. No two are the same, even when they have the same personality type. That said, there are two things I would like you to do. First, understand that you can't generalize or stereotype the four major personality types. Don't say, "All Fire-type personalities are all the same!" That would not be true. That's like saying all football teams are the same because they're football teams, or that all cars are alike. You get the point. There is a lot to be considered. People and their personalities are like having many cooks in the kitchen, remove or add one, and the menu changes. Another factor is the choices. The choices we make carry consequences that make us respond by creating other necessary choices. You understand this already. You have heard others say, "If you tell a lie, you will have to tell another to cover that one." In this example, the first lie makes it necessary to tell the next.

As the leader and supplier of vision and focus in your home, the second thing I need you to do is find the areas where you and your wife can grow and write them down. Keep in mind that just because you're the head doesn't mean you force your wife to make a change. I heard it said, the man may be the head, but the wife is the neck that turns the head. Sooner or later, she will get around to turning your point of view. It is a chance for you to work together.

Your wife, just like you, is growing. This means she isn't finished yet. She isn't a finished product, and you aren't a finished product either. Sometimes we act as if we are complete and perfect in every way. The beauty of marriage is that two people come together to live, experience new things, and out of it all, you grow closer, wiser, and more in love as time goes on.

As the head, you must master your domain. You don't have to know everything, just what you need to know. Studying you're, and your wife's personality type is part of what you need to know. So, as you begin to read about different personality types, their habits, love expectations, relationship skills, and so on, you will have to pick and choose from the information you are about to read and piece together what you think is or is not like your wife. The same goes for you and your personality type. People are not "One size fits all," and neither will their personalities. At the same time, you should also leave a little room for growth. Consider that even though something doesn't seem like your wife (or yourself), ask if it could be true. Leave room also for the unknown.

You are not the only one playing this game. The truth is, your wife has a number of unspoken desires just like you do. Finally, think about some of the things your wife has told you in past conversations, joking around, or even arguing. Deeper truths could be staring you in the face.

I also have to say, stop expecting perfection from her. (Don't worry, if your wife is reading the companion version of this book, I'm telling him the same thing about you! I got your back!) You may not be, but it's always good to remind husbands that their wives are just as scared, insecure, and unsure about many things just like they are. Add to that feeling insecure about weight, shape, hips, age, and wrinkles, and you have the perfect setting for making many mistakes and imperfections.

Each personality type's finances, communication, stress, and sex & intimacy habits will be introduced to you. See your own, then try to see your wife's.

Finances and Personality

Finances are critical to a family. Couples who argue over finances are said to have a higher risk of breaking up. It's not sex, family, or communication; but finances. This is why you must understand how your wife's personality may deal with financial issues.

Earth Strengths

Stop and think of how you are with finances. Are you solid or shaky when it comes to dealing with money? When it comes to finances, the Earth Personality can be just as dependable as the earth itself. When it comes to taking care of financial business, the Earth Personality says, "It has to be done right!" And yes, they have the definition of what right means. In finances, their perfectionist talents go to work. Calculating to the penny and accounting for every nickel gives them a sense of pride.

Many men leave financial matters to "The Mrs." because they don't want to be bothered. Watch how your wife pays for an item and then consider how you perform the same task. Balancing a checkbook is practically a "must" for the Earth Type Personality simply because it is the right thing to do. Because they tend to be a little on the pessimistic and even distrusting side, they imagine that literally, anything could happen to the money. A bank teller could type a wrong number in and reduce the accounts balance, or someone could grab the receipt that wasn't properly disposed of and steal your identity and money. As an Earth Personality, they take pride in their precise calculations, often balancing the checkbook to the penny. "The Earth" man or woman delights in comparing the checkbook to the bank statement.

Investments? Investing will never happen without a lot of research. Don't even think about it. If you are an Earth Personality, you may be tempted to laugh because you know it's true. With the Earth Personality type, its either analysis or paralysis. Nothing happens without gathering information, a lot of information. The Earth Personality must do research, extensive research. In their eyes, not a penny is to be invested unless all the pertinent facts have been gathered, reviewed, evaluated, revisited, reworked, and rehashed. For the Earth Personality, each project is a NASA moon launch. A simple dinner outing wouldn't be complete without tallying up the bill. After all, the waitress or waiter could have made a mistake.

Let an Earth Personality handle your bills. Want good credit? This is not to say that every Earth Personality has good credit, but they have the skill set. I'm simply saying they can easily make it happen, more than many other types if they choose to. It is their meticulous attention to details that make them great accountants and CFO's.

Earth personalities are not the kind that easily bends to shifty salespeople; they are not emotional or compulsive buyers. They can allow certain purchases if it falls within their budget and for a predetermined and planned item, or luxury. Even if they agree to purchase an item, it still has to be the "right" item and at the "right" price.

Earth Weaknesses
You may say, "I Love My Wife But… when it comes to money, she's cheap, expects me to keep receipts, and balance the checkbook to the penny!"

You remember the story of the tortoise and the hare. Your wife is not the hare in finances. She will move slower, and when a situation calls for quick impulse buying or investing, you can expect resistance. They may even refuse entirely and let you deal with the consequences, washing their hands of the situation. Why? Simply because it wasn't done the right way. The Earth Personalities believe, on some level, that everyone should operate or at least understand that their way is the best way to handle such things, especially finances.

Even when trying to enjoy a purchase, the Earth Personality tends to bring up possible negatives or may say something to dampen the happy purchasing occasion.

Strategy
Your Earth Personality wife needs to know that you appreciate her sharp eye and frugal habits. Let her know that she balances you. Ask her why she thinks the purchase or financial move is the best. After she tells you, give her affirmation and praise, which makes her reason for the fun and happy purchase or investment. Be thankful and rest easy knowing she's on the job.

~

Air Strengths
Air Personalities are often the best sales associates to hire. Their personality types can easily see the benefits of purchasing, having, or spending on a particular

item. The check is always on its way, and they will get to balancing the checkbook someday, maybe. Unlike the Earth Personality who reaches for the bank statement, they do just the opposite. "Okay, whatever, I don't have time to deal with that now, I'll just check the balance later." The Air Personality "Thinks" they have enough in the bank, and that's all that matters. Thinking more about how they will look in the new suit, jeans, or car far outweighs anything else. As far as the finances and payments go, "It'll be okay; it's going to be fine, I get paid in a couple of weeks." You have to love his optimism.

Air Personalities are open to financial suggestions as long as they don't have to follow it as a rule, and it helps their image. If it's fun and enjoyable, these personality types are open to new things and ideas. They see the advantage of spending, investing, and taking a chance. They are the right choice for supporting a purchase, an investment, or even a gamble. Just don't ask them where the checkbook is or about tracking their budget. Just tell him the money is in the account, and he may not mind you buying shoes and a purse to match.

Air Weaknesses

You could say, "I Love My Wife But… when it comes to finances, I have to do everything, or we are late paying the bills."

Your Air wife is disorganized when it comes to balancing a checkbook, keeping up with statements, and keeping a bill payment calendar. She often goes by what she feels when it comes to finances instead of the facts. Not only in finances, but she is disorganized when it comes to meticulous details and hates bits and pieces of papers and things that must be kept and organized.

Strategy
Understand that her personality style is about freedom, fun, friends, and fixing herself up to enjoy any one of those. The pure Air Personality would not make the best accountant or CFO unless they have a strong secondary personality trait like Earth or Fire. This is not to say that your Air wife can't work things out. You would be surprised to know that just thinking of one's credit rating as social status or money not saved taking away from a nice vacation can have a significant effect on an Air Personality. Remember, if put in the right context, the Air Personality can make the adjustments to get what it wants.

Your Air wife wants to do better and will even have a conversation with you about it. She may feel responsible for leading her family to better financial places than what she has done in the past. When left to herself, her credit rating may be challenged with a few dings here and there (okay, a lot!). The necessary skills to balance the checkbook and pay bills on time must be put in terms she understands - luxury and leisure. Doing what is necessary should lead to a reward of purchasing a vacation or something that she has had her eye on. For her, the task must end in something enjoyable, fun, or satisfying.

~

Fire Strengths

Like its Air cousin, Fire can be impatient and unable to wait for natural processes to yield results. This means that if you want something done as soon as possible, give it to a Fire Personality. No time to wait, no time to discuss it fully, "Let's just do it already!" The Fire Personality is a "Take the bull by the horns" kind of person who blows their horn a half-second before the light turns green! They are the kind of person that brings that same strength and decisiveness to finances. As task-oriented as his Earth cousin, the Fire Personality likes to get things done. Keep in mind that your Fire wife may be able to take charge, but her vision and understanding include the overall picture and not details.

Do not expect a bank statement to be gone over with a fine-toothed comb. Understand that the bottom line or conclusion is all she wants. Your Fire wife has a gift that sums up an entire situation, concludes what should be done, and creates a plan of action in no time. As a visionary, she can quickly think up a financial goal and then create a plan for doing what it takes to get there. She feels that with your cooperation, she can move the world. Financially, she has the strength to budget and stick to it, as long as she doesn't create a reason not to.

Always thinking ahead of the game, she has a good idea of which bills are due. Her mind is constantly going, and the family finances are a part of her focus. It has to be because she has other things to do that require money. She has all the confidence in the world that she can control the finances. She will often attempt to strike out on a venture or tangent in hopes of increasing financial standing. She always wants more even though and is always growing, moving, thinking, and finding reasons to strike out on new plans.

Fire Weaknesses

You may say, "I Love My Wife But.... when it comes to finances, she doesn't care how others feel, she just goes and does what she thinks is best without me!"

Remember, "Take the bull by the horns" kind of person. That's what your Fire wife is. You love it when things have to get done. The thing is, she doesn't turn off, and there is not an off switch. Just give her some Air in the form of happy fun, inspiration, or even deep conversation, and she's ready. Fire can be bull-headed, not listening to anyone about anything, including finances. The Fire Personality has to have a cause, a reason. This is both good and bad. Having a budget is good, but when the Fire Personality thinks of her "Cause" or many projects and ideas she has, she sees no problem investing in them. After all, she is going to make it happen! She has no problem seeing the glass half full, and she's ready to pay for her share because she truly believes a full glass is coming. Yes, it's because she's going to make it happen! Did I say she was going to make it happen?

Strategy

Understand, your fire wife drive is to accomplish something. Her Fire Personality is goal-oriented and will dig in and not budge, to save the world. It often has to be her way or the highway. This personality is task and goal-oriented. Like her Earth cousin, she wants results. Like her Air cousin also, she isn't concerned about the particulars because she is often making it up as she goes. She's creative that way.

There are two things your Fire wife may feel threatened by. The first threat is time, "There never seems to be enough time to finish!" The second threat is progress and accomplishment. She's wired to listen for things that will help her get things done quicker, better, and on a higher level. This gives you an opportunity to suggest a desired direction or change by asking, "Wouldn't it get you to your goal quicker if..?" or "If we did this….we would really be able to get things done and go to the next level!"

Remember, your Fire wife needs to get results; how she gets them is secondary. With Fire being aggressive, they are often thought of as controlling. This means she may want her way and think her way is right, even though you suggest otherwise. Don't be shaken. Just give your Fire wife some Air in the form of inspiration, reason, and tell her that you believe in her, Fire likes warm conversations and actions. Give her a hug, but just don't hug her for too long, she has to go do something.

~

Water Strengths

If you have a Water Wife, you have one of the most supportive personality types. When it comes to finances, she shows great strengths in being able to save patiently. She has no problem saving for a rainy day, which never seems to come, so she keeps saving. She may comfortably put a hundred dollars into a savings account every payday without even missing a beat. This is simply amazing to the Air Personality, smart to the Earth Personality, and admirable to the Fire Personality. As Air thinks about what they could spend it on, and Earth thinks about how it's great planning to save for a rainy day, and Fire thinks about what they could do with it, Water just moves happily along, just thankful to be back home from the bank in time for dinner.

Budgeting and balancing the checkbook is something they leave for someone else. They will try it and try to do a good job if it helps or makes everything better. Don't expect your Water wife to dress like a peacock or show off like a model. When it comes to purchasing, they are comfortable as long as it isn't too much or too flashy, or something that will draw attention. Water Personalities are "go with the flow" kind of people; they greatly support the other personality types that show an intense drive.

Water Weaknesses

You may say, "I Love My Wife But...she doesn't have a preference, whatever I want to do with the money is usually okay, what is our goal?"

Okay, look, I can see that sometimes you want more drive and initiative out of your supportive wife. Keep in mind; you are attracted to her qualities because of what you don't have and what you share at the same time. You don't want her pulling in one direction and you in another. I know, "At least it would be fun to play and sometimes have opposition." Save that for the basketball court. You are blessed to have someone who is in your corner. Many men pray for a wife like yours.

Your Water wife will often hold back her thoughts and go with yours. That means if you say you wish to go in a certain direction, she will usually say, "Okay." They may know what is best but usually will not speak up until pressed to say something. Finances between husbands and wives need to be discussed, and opinions stated. Here is where the Water Personality may suffer because they refuse to rock the boat.

Often passive, the Water Personality prefers to vote behind the scenes. Because they are beings of consistency, they prefer to get on a path that works and stay with it regardless. You can argue about how great it would be to change as they smile, nod, and not change anything. In investing, they prefer a solid and sure thing, not given to chance or recklessness. Your Water wife isn't a chance taker. If you need a spontaneous and right now kind of investor, this may not be the right person for you. Next to the Air Personality, they are the next profitable target for persuasive sales pitches. Flowing with different levels of emotion, they often use finances as a gauge of how much they will go along with your program or not.

Strategy
Water wants everything to be all right and everyone to be happy. Like their Fire cousins, they can easily see the big picture when it comes to doing what is best for others' wellbeing. They are huge supporters and will get behind you and do the work. To empower them to lead in the area of finances, they must be convinced that at the present time, it's the best choice for everyone involved if things keep going smoothly. Water makes a good friend to Earth and feels much better when you communicate the reasons for the need and how to get things done.

Take A Moment

Take out your Wish-List and match the characteristics of your wishes with the kind of person needed. Would a Fire, Air, Earth, or Water person be best?

Look at your answer from the "Your Element" chapter and see if you are the type needed for the job. If you are, any discomfort in this area is you simply trying to sculpt your wife in your own image. Let her be herself. Perhaps you should take over the finances, discuss it. If you both fit, then make it a together moment as you work on finances.

Communication and Personality

Effective communication between you and your mate is key to meeting each other's needs. Problems in communication also rank high among reasons couples divorce. Communication helps you resolve the conflict by communicating fairly and listening intently to what your mate is saying.

Earth Strengths
"I have embarrassed myself," is a thought, your Earth wife knows well. She doesn't want to embarrass herself or make a fool of herself, especially in public. Like the Earth, the communication style is both thoughtful and deliberate. Not thoughtful as in, "Wow, how nice you were thinking of me..." but the other kind of thoughtful. I'm talking about having a head full of thoughts - competing thoughts. Your Earth wife thinks a lot but wonders even more, "Should I have said that, done that, what about this?"

The Earth Personality has many thoughts, but they have even more questions than thoughts or conclusions. The Earth Personality is often unsure about themselves and would love to take the time to research and study themselves if only it weren't so psychologically intense and emotionally challenging. Their faces rarely show the depth of what they feel, even though they don't know what they feel at times. Your Earth wife may be in the habit of feeling what she wants and thinks, instead of talking aloud. This means she can be very passionate as we will discuss later, but also that she spends a lot of time in her own head and may think something is right that isn't. Help her feel accepted and wonderful just as she is.

Your Earth wife is likely to think, "He knows I love him; I don't have to say it all the time." Their style of communication is very deliberate, and don't let their dry sense of humor bring you to tears of laughter. Sometimes giving their humor a little pause makes it funny. When your Earth wife says something humorous, give it five seconds, and it will become funny. Often not speaking very much, they say what has to be said and then quickly stops as if to say, "I'm glad that's over." On the phone, they can seem quick and to the point while giving the impression that they really didn't want to speak to you when in reality they did, because they just spoke to you. Do not expect a bubbly response or a warm and deep smile. Like their Fire cousins, the point is appreciated and should be gotten too quickly. Chances are you will never find an Earth Personality in idle chatter on the telephone for hours.

Earth Weaknesses

You are the one that wanted to "Keep it Real!" If that's what you wanted, then you have the right person. You can count on your Earth wife to usually tell it like it is when you can get her to say what's on her heart. Consider her a realist or even a pessimist who will share with you the reality of how things are. Unfortunately, it turns out to be the reality of her world, which is usually a little negative. As you know already, she can be extremely literal, picking at words and meanings to the letter, and often reminding you of what you said in past conversations. No, she didn't write it down or record it, but you would think she did.

Self-doubt and questioning are no stranger to your Earth wife. She asks herself questions like, "Am I going too far with this? Am I sharing too much information? Am I wrong about this?" Her world is a world of factual puzzle pieces that must fit together without a problem. If there is a problem, then there will have to be a reckoning. She won't leave that issue alone until the puzzle pieces are safely put where it belongs.

If you have an Earth wife, I know you have experienced this. You made a mistake; she brought it to your attention. You later showed her you "got it" by doing things her way only to find out she still sees you as doing the same thing even though you showed her you could do differently. This is because she has to see consistency, once doesn't do it for her. She has to know that the problem is solved for good, which takes time.

Strategy
Your Earth wife may seem hard to move in some cases and even stoic or rigid. Don't be fooled. As you know, she has a lot of passion and fire within her, just as the Earth does at its core. She can be compassionate and emotional, even though it may never be fully communicated. Just as her face may never show

emotional depth, her mouth may not speak it either. Just know that it's there. To deal with and persuade your Earth wife, you need to be patient and simply communicate the reason for a given move, need, or facts. Before receiving what you want from her, it's always best to give information first, constantly affirming and valuing her verbally or subtly. Remember, the Earth gently turns on its axis as gravity keeps everything and everyone grounded. This is like your wife, who doesn't want to be jarred with any sudden moves she hasn't had time to prepare for.

~

Air Strengths
Just as air is needed for us to talk to one another, the Air wife thrives on communication. She loves to talk and can talk about anything at any time. If ever there was an area of strength for the Air Personality, communication is IT! The gift of gab is worked overtime with this one. Your Air wife has absolutely no problem holding a conversation with anyone and makes a great storyteller. Whether the story is true or fabricated, she is sure to remain the party's life for telling it. She is a true "people" person. This is great for her because socially, she can be a rock star. As a people person, she loves to interact with people and may feel the need to just be around others. She has to mingle, mix, and talk about whatever is on her mind. She would make a great orator, minister, salesperson, teacher, or even customer service representative.

She may never meet a stranger and seem bold and unafraid to speak in public or before large groups of people. For this reason, the Air wife makes friends and can kid around with perfect strangers so easily. Many people like Air Personalities for all the reasons above.

If in a debate, the Air Personality can battle like no other. If you need to be verbally defended, an Air Personality is just the type you need on your side. They make the best lawyers, actors, and politicians. This personality type can also be very quick on their feet and provide answers where none exist. As good storytellers, they can be very creative in communication. I have experienced Air Personalities making up whole stories and scenarios out of thin air.

They are also good at negotiating and finding a happy medium for any two sides. They are born diplomats and can easily manipulate or deceive of they decide to use their gift for the wrong causes. Like Air dances and is free to go in either direction, the Air Personality wants to be free to express itself just because it feels like doing so. Your wife wants to be free to communicate what she feels and thinks.

Air Weaknesses

You may say, "I Love My Wife, but she shares too much of our information with others, doesn't know when to be quiet, and is 'flirty' to other men!"

Let's face it. There have been times when you thought your wife was a little too friendly or comfortable with some of the fellas you brought by. She doesn't intend to be too friendly, but you know she can be. When you notice it, it bothers you and an argument or two later; you wonder if something is going on. Just because she doesn't meet strangers, makes friends easily, and can start conversations from dead silence, doesn't mean that she is flirty or unfaithful. She is a light-hearted and friendly soul that is simply trying to enjoy life and the world around her. If you notice, she is just as friendly with women as she is with men.

Strategy

How do you really get through to your Air wife? She loves stories. Her way of communicating is through stories. Think back on some of your conversations. Remember how you would sometime be annoyed by her taking a long way around and giving you examples rather than just saying what she wants? She is wired for communicating through stories. Engage her through stories and make her feel as if she has 100% of your attention. She has to know that you would rather be doing nothing else than listening to her and enjoying the moment. Your Air wife is a select group that makes some of the best actors, lawyers, negotiators, politicians, and diplomats. Most of all, she wants to have fun and enjoy life with you.

~

Fire Strengths

"Make it happen!" Take control of the situation and declare what your future is going to be! These are saying to live by for your Fire wife. In communication, the same thing is true. She often feels like telling you to, "Spit it out already!" or "Just say what you want!" She looks at things in a big picture view and boils everything down to a simple understanding of a few words. "That's all there is to it!"

She prefers to be communicated with brief and to-the-point statements because that is all that is needed. This is why the Fire Personality can be short on a conversation unless it is meaningful. That usually means the things that she's working on or thinking about. She has things to do and wants to make progress at any cost. The last thing she wants to do is be stuck in a conversation that isn't going anywhere. It's not that she doesn't want to talk; she only wants to talk about the relevant things.

Fire Weaknesses

You may say, "I Love My Wife But...she often says things that hurt my feelings and put her projects before family and me all the time."

Your Fire wife is the kind of person that will ask what others are thinking but too afraid to ask. She is bold, sometimes too bold, and can be very confrontational if she is sure that her cause is right. She can be the classic bull in the china shop. Your Fire wife has shown you the ability to take the lead and handle things. I don't have to tell you that your Fire wife can be stubborn, you know this. She is a "Go-

Getter" and arises to the challenge and often refuses to back down from almost any challenge.

Her strength in time of adversity and achieving goals is equal to her insensitivity and unwillingness to budge, even emotionally. She knows there will be sacrifices. To accomplish things, she may feel like there must be emotional sacrifices that you must make, just as she has already made her sacrifices. Like tensing up in preparation for being hit, she has already made the necessary adjustments to get the job done. She is only asking you to do what she's already done. She may feel as if it will all be worth it, and you'll even thank her afterward, but you just don't see it right now.

One problem is that fire can warm, but it also burns. In passion for the vision, leaping to the next level, and she powerfully felts even intimacy. As you know, your Fire wife can passionately win an argument with ease. You wouldn't want to half-heartedly challenge unless you were loaded with ammunition and ready to fire first and often - bring a lunch. Remember, fire burns. There may be times when you feel as if you can't get through to this bull-headed Fire Personality. Trust me; she's considering what you said even if she doesn't show it or act on it. If she just gives in, it may seem like some sort of weakness or lack of ability. She'll change, just not right in front of you. It has to be on her terms. She is built to dominate, which means she has to be in control, often.

Strategy
Depending on your marriage model, she may either look at you as an equal, as the head or, as someone, she has to "help." Regardless, try to understand her vision, quest, goal, or whatever she's trying to do. Understand that her desire to take control has nothing to do with you; it's the way she is wired and how she deals with life and living. Control, domination, and making swift moves is how she operates. Considering your Fire wife, remember, it's easier to steer a fire truck from inside it than outside it. Your challenge is to see where her vision will take the family and deal with reality from her perspective and timetable. From there, you can ask, suggest, even question in a way that gets more results than fighting. When she senses a battle, she takes it as a treat to her ability to make progress and be effective. She will then work to gain more control. You don't want that.

~

Water Strengths
Water can be a shallow pool or a deep ocean. Its waves can be calm or rough. This also describes the potential of your Water wife in communication. Still, waters may run deep. How do you know you have a deep one on your hands? If she loves poetry and wants to talk about emotions and feelings, then you have a deep one. If she looks at normal situations and finds something interesting to pull out of it, then yes, you have a deep one. If she isn't, then her communication, I am on the

shallow side of the pool. On the shallow end is gossip, what someone is wearing or should be, or any other surface conversation that doesn't mean that much.

Regardless of which end, she is in, shallow or deep, she thinks and feels more than she may ever tell you. Like her Earth cousin, she can keep her true cards close to her chest, only letting them out when it's absolutely necessary. As the classic passive-aggressive, she may never say anything but rather prove what she's thinking and feeling by what she does, or even more than that, what she refuses to do.

She thinks before she speaks and is aware of what to say and not say. She could be offended talking with you, and you may never know it. She prefers you not to say anything at all if you don't mean it. She has to trust that what you are saying is sincere. If she suspects you are not trustworthy and truthful, she may never trust you again while still speaking to you. She doesn't want to hurt your feelings regardless of what she is feeling.

Trust what she says because she is sincere and takes you at your word. She speaks calmly and is non-confrontational. She is all about peace and everything being all-right and wants to be sure before she responds. She doesn't want to offend and may just go with the flow for peace's sake.

Water Weaknesses
You may say, "I Love My Wife But... she doesn't have enough ambition or motivation. It's like she has no goals and settles for anything - she's too easy-going."

You have to remember who you're dealing with here. She is water. Think about how hard it would be to move Lake Michigan. She is just as likely not to be moved by a suggestion, a command, or even a discussion. She has to get into the flow, feel the new direction, and let things happen naturally, not forced. Things have to be in place and ready for change. She doesn't like to change otherwise. She finds safety in numbers and in whatever everyone else says is ok.

She is a part of a select group that just so happens to make up 60 to 80% of the planet. As part of those who make visions come to pass through their cooperation and hard work, she is supportive and your best ally. Don't expect her to take the bull by the horns or lead the pack. The background is where she thrives. She is happy to support you and help you get what you need to make a difference. Cherish this.

Strategy
The last thing you would want to do is be confrontational and argumentative with her. She is already willing and able to help you by giving you what you need. There is no need to create an atmosphere of contention, strife, and bickering. She is self-controlled and does not need to be dominated. What she needs most is acceptance, validation, and patience. Remember, she doesn't like to be moved suddenly or repeatedly. Calmly communicate your vision, plans, and goals in a calm and peaceful way, and all will be well. She knows you are the man when you give her

what she needs and communicates what you want her to do or how you want her to help. She will not try to outshine you, conspire against you, or respond negatively to you unless she feels consistently provoked. You have a good thing here, don't let your insecurity ruin it for you.

Note: Check yourself. If you have tried to dominate her rather than cooperate with her, you are shooting yourself in the foot. If you yell and intimidate her, you are causing unnecessary pain that you will end up paying for. She needs a loving leader, not a dominating slave driver.

Take A Moment

Take out your Wish-List and match the characteristics of your wishes with the kind of person needed. Would a Fire, Air, Earth, or Water person be best? Ask your wife to share her element with you if she hasn't done so already. No matter what element she is, you can help her by doing the following:

<u>If she is Fire</u>: First praise her for how she has communicated with you. Then, show her your vision of how things could be better if she communicated a certain way. Share how it would make you feel, and help you in the long run.

If she is Air: Share with her how you enjoy her lively spirit and sharing with her. Then, share with her that you would really enjoy ( ) kind of sharing more often.

If she is Water: Let her know everything is just fine and that you are happy at home with her. Then, encourage her and let her know you really need ( ) kind of communication or more of it.

If she is Earth: Give her a big hug and tell her, I want more communication between us.

Stress and Personality

Okay, what doesn't kill you makes you stronger right? That's actually not true, and there are proven studies that suggest stress can kill you. If stress can kill a person, it can, without a doubt, kill a marriage. You have to know how to manage stress according to your personality and your wife's personality.

Earth Strengths
Who likes stress? Which type of personality deals with stress the best? One type has found a way of deflecting stress altogether and just laugh it off. Another type meets it head-on and refuses to back down while using it to soar higher. Yet another style retreats from stress and even may avoid it like the ostrich hiding its head in the sand. And then there's the other type that has the ability to become so agitated with the stress that they may literally burn themselves out thinking up a

solution to deal with it. For the Earth wife, stress and the demands of having to make quick decisions presents a new threat all by itself. It is a problem in addition to the actual problem. Stress alone builds up like an emotional time-bomb that causes the Earth wife to become agitated, angry, or to panic.

The only thing worse than such a problem to the Earth wife is the thought of having caused the problem. She thinks that if she has caused the problem, then she is missing key information that she somehow overlooked. That is another big problem. When she thinks that she has opened the door to this problem by not foreseeing what was ahead of her or around her, it makes things even worse.

One thing that helps is her ability to keep calm enough to think about things and make decisions before completely breaking down. In stress, she is busy thinking of ways to understand and solve the problem. She needs to see where the problem came from and understand the complete process of how this new challenge was created and how it can be solved. She is stressed and won't be the same until things are resolved. She will work things out, given enough time, research, and support from you.

Earth Weaknesses
You may say, "I Love My Wife But... when things go bad, she thinks the worst and almost goes into depression when I need her most!"

Because perfection is her goal, she often kicks herself to not live up to the standards she blames the world for not having. Seeking to control what she can not only frustrate her further. After realizing the world isn't such a bad place after attempting to look at things on the bright side, she momentarily snaps out of it until the present situation reminds her. Control can and often does become an issue; it's how she deals with the uncertainty of the world. This may only cause her to sink deeper into her own little world with its self-imposed emergencies and unattainable standards. When your wife takes things personally, she may internalize her failure. To cope, you find her spending more time alone and licking her wounds in quietness. She mentally and emotionally punishes herself, thinking she should have known better or known that this would or could happen.

Your wife has a gift for hearing that inner voice of reason. It gives her the ability to calculate and come up with solutions to problems. This same voice also becomes a problem when she becomes the focus or problem. Often feeling that something about her isn't good enough, she can easily and quickly be down on herself about the smallest thing.

Strategy
Just like the planet itself, Earth has many places of beauty and danger; it has hostile and pleasant climates. Your Earth wife is the same in many ways. She has to be affirmed and reassured that you need all

that she brings to the table. She has to know that you are patiently waiting for her to resolve whatever issue she feels is important. Let her know that she has all the time in the world. Remind her the glass is half full and that she has been victorious in the past and has what it takes to succeed. Just keep this in mind; she doesn't like to be smothered with insincere inspiration or motivation. Simple and sweet is best. Don't overdo it.

~

Air Strengths

The first response to stress by your Air wife, maybe, "I hate this!" "I can't stand this!" When it's time to deal with it, your Air wife will find a way to either make light of it or joke about it or even remember a story about a friend that had a similar situation. Your Air wife may deal with stress by completely avoiding it altogether or meeting it head-on by making a joke out of it.

She would make a good stand-up comedian. Just like her Water cousin, stress may be avoided altogether. The only thing is, Air will have a party to make up for it. It has to be fun and exciting. Easily bored, even stress has to bow its knee to her light and airy ways of fun and humor. Without fun and funny, she is no party at all, and she feels completely out of her element. She understands that life isn't always a party, but that doesn't mean you can't still laugh a little.

She knows how to cheer you up when you're down and how to turn the tables on stress and problems. Over the years, she has learned how to handle them because she often brings stress and problems through consistent procrastination, overspending, and lack of details. She is resilient and can force a smile through just about anything. When all fails, she can easily cheer herself up by contacting a girlfriend to go window shopping, on a spending spree, or get coffee.

Air Weaknesses
You may say, "I Love My Wife But... she doesn't take problems seriously and doesn't take care of business as she should!"

One of your wife's greatest assets is in the brightness she brings to the room and the silver lining in the clouds she owns. To say it a different way, she is naturally positive and optimistic. Because she is all of this and a bag of chips, she is often naive when it comes to dire circumstances. Making little of great problems is excellent when you need to motivate someone but not when you have to deal with reality and face problems head-on. She does take problems seriously, but she just goes about it in a way that seems uncaring or not as bad or serious as it really is. The problem is, it just maybe that bad or worse. Her constant thought is, "Everything is going to be fine; I'll get to it later."

As an Air personality, your wife is a good communicator, and she feels like she can talk her way in and out of situations. It's a gift. She may not be able to talk her way out of everything, but she certainly can make things better.

You have seen her create stress in her life by waiting too long to handle important business, talking too long, or fellowshipping longer than needed as important things wait. You are a good husband as you remind her of what is waiting, important bills and dates, and help her find her keys again. You may sometimes get a laugh out of her talking to herself as much as she does; it's just her way of thinking aloud. No, she's not crazy (at least not yet!)

Strategy

Okay, here is where you may be able to learn something from your wife in the way she deals with stress. She seems to have a shield that protects her from things like stress. You know that she cares but, she often appears not to care at all as she laughs it off and says everything is going to be fine. To a certain degree, she's right. Everything is going to be alright, as long as things are tended to in a business manner.

If you communicate with her by showing her everything negative and wrong, she will think you are trying to pull her down. If you continue to point out how she is responsible, or the cause of the problem, she will begin to think you are her problem. Don't spend time trying to convict her or shame her. This drives her away from you instead of toward you. Instead, understand the atmosphere she needs and work from there.

How? Help her to develop a work first attitude. You may start this on a Saturday if she has them off. Have a conversation with her on Friday that there's something fun you want to do on Saturday with her but that there are things to do early Saturday morning. Let this be the start of your emphasizing a "Work first, then play all day" mindset. Over time, this will help her take care of business first and then have the time to play and talk as much as she wants.

~

Fire Strengths

I heard it said that an eagle could chart a storm a hundred miles away and aim right for it. When entering the storm, it locks its wings in the maximum climb position and is quickly shot above it to soar with the storm beneath him. This is a good description of how your Fire wife deals with stress. She may view it as a challenge, but she needs it and often creates a climate of stress to get things done.

Put your Fire wife in a stressful challenge, and she becomes a noble warrior whose cause is just and right! She refuses to give in or back down as tensions rise. In these moments, you would think she could leap tall buildings in a single bound and also bounce bullets off her chest. It's true that she seems to get extra strength from somewhere and proves it by staying up late and rising early. She will let nothing get in her way of progress and success. What makes things even worse for the problem is that she has a mind that can think up strategies on the fly and develop plans while her feet are running toward the problem. That problem doesn't stand a chance; it's going down. As you know, she is very imaginative and creative. She is best when she is thinking on her feet.

This adds to her level of stress and sends her into overdrive. It feeds her with a kind of rush. Whatever you do, don't get in her way at this point. She's a loaded locomotive that is running full speed ahead.

Speaking of speed, she needs a certain pace. Things have to flow at a certain speed for her; fast is usually best. This is why she often walks as if she's going to put out a fire. For this reason, you may also say, "I Love My Wife But, she is so impatient and is always wanting to rush me. I'm can never move or talk quickly enough for her!" This is just her pace for getting things done, and a means for her to be inspired. When she asks you to move quicker or, "Hurry Up!" she is only asking that you help her with the environment she needs for motivation. She simply wants to know you are with her. Your speed demonstrates that you are with her in getting results quickly. This is the world she lives in, and she's glad you are in it. Never forget, though, she needs results, and the sooner she gets them, the better. She wanted everything yesterday.

As a man, you may feel a little intimidated when you try to lead someone that seems to be already ahead of the game. With your Fire wife, you lead her by what she feeds on. Stress will pop up on its own, and at times Fire needs that. Where you begin to lead, is in what she truly needs - Air. Without Air, Fire dies every time. Fire needs the Air of inspiration, affirmation, confidence, and assurance from loving arms.

Fire Weaknesses
You may say, "I Love My Wife But... she is too driven. She creates three more projects before the last one is done. It's like she's always thinking of what's next and never rests."

The nature of Fire, in real life, shows that it has a way of not burning everything in its path, it skips things from time to time. This is true of your Fire wife. She is optimistic, and like her Air cousin who feeds her, she feels everything will be okay. As fire skips, your Fire wife may skip necessary steps or rules needed for her success. Because she is driven, she feels she can make just about any situation work.

The problem here is that it may take a while for her to realize that force is not the answer. It's good to have confidence in your ability to handle things, but sometimes you have to listen to reality. Situations will later scream at her, "This isn't working!" Because she's always in a hurry and fatally optimistic, she doesn't have time to hear that now even though it will haunt her later. A critical time for her is when she sits for a moment and reflects on how much progress she hasn't made, and any failures she's made.

Her element is Fire, which consumes. Her environment is Air, and her focus is on things to do and consume. Her posture is leaning into the wind as she gains ground, makes progress, and takes names. One of her greatest challenges is in losing time, momentum, and progress altogether. Realizing that she is in the same place year after year is a nightmare for her. She may be a little regretful or remorseful for not accomplishing what she set out to while in High School.

All of this serves her. She has what it takes to use even the stress she creates for herself. Like the eagle, she can chart a storm and be propelled higher, even if it's a storm she created for herself.

Strategy

Here is a secret for you alone. Your Fire wife isn't stressed out by stress but fueled by it, as long as it's not overwhelming, by her standards. Fire can take more heat than any, but there comes a time when even Fire feels the heat or even gets burned. Your Fire wife needs to see results and make progress, and when that doesn't happen, she takes it personally. All your Fire Wife needs is resourcefulness and a dream, or a cause. If you think she is stressing herself out, know that it is because she isn't getting the results she would like, and she needs a little more push, a little more energy to solve the problem.

What she loves receiving gifts and pointers that increase her ability to produce. Point her attention to the resources she has or even talk about her vision or dream. Remind her that she will make it and then help her with resources and resourcefulness to use what she has to its fullest.

When you need her to shift a little, address whatever changes you think need to be made. The only thing is you should put them in a context that helps her accomplish her goals. If you think she is too hard on everyone, suggest that the family can help her and take some of a load of if she would work with instead of against. She'll understand that progress means working together rather than fussing at one or two people.

She will greatly appreciate you co-signing her dream or cause and admire you for it. The best strategy for dealing with this type of personality is to remind them of their dream, point them to their resources, help, or just get out of their way.

~

Water Strengths

Have you ever tried to boil the ocean or even a swimming pool? Or how about trying to boil a pot of water with a single match. It won't work. Many times, it takes just as long to boil a pot of water with a single match as it does to get a Water wife boiling mad. It is not impossible to get them angry; it just takes a while. There are always those special cases where you hit the right nerve and get a quick reaction; we all do that. But to get your Water wife truly angry takes work.

That is nothing to shout about. Like his Earth cousin, when Water is finally moved to an emotional place, it can be very difficult to get them to move away from that place, or offense. They remember what you did and said and are just as moved by it today as they were then and will be in the future. This classic passive-aggressive personality acts out on its decisions by not doing what instead of setting your car on Fire. While your Water wife makes the greatest helpmate and ally on Earth, putting her in a place of distrust, fear, and intimidation will always come back to bite you. Water will always win over the long run because it can patiently drown Earth, suffocate Air, and quench Fire just by calmly being what it is, Water. As one of the more low-key elements, its power is in simply being.

As high winds can cause waves to become violent, so does the wrong kind of thinking or inspiration stir up your Water wife; still waters do run deep, deep with reasons to either stick by you or abandon you, but you may never know the full reason why. They are non-confrontational and are more than likely to side-step stress altogether.

Your Water wife flows best with easy-going settings where the love and endearment of family and friends are felt deeply. Even in moments of stress, their loyalties remain true as long as they are convinced it's the right thing to do and the right way to be. Water Personalities make the best friends and may never let you know they are angry with you unless pushed over the edge.

Water Weaknesses

You may say, "I Love My Wife But... nothing I say or do moves her. It's too hard to get her going, and she only stays motivated for a short time!"

Your Water wife may not have ever heard these words spoken by Bruce Lee, but she takes this philosophy seriously. She is concerned about everyone's comfort, including her own, but feels no need to make herself fit any mold or model that makes her uncomfortable. Things being comfortable on a deeper level is most important to her emotionally, psychologically, and spiritually. Like her Earth cousin, stress is felt a little deeper than with other personality types. Stress brings tension in the Air and makes things unbearable for her.

In stress, she will want to stick to what has worked in the past. Proven techniques and patterns are always her choice way of dealing with things. She would rather sit tight, do nothing, and let things blow over than try something new and unproven. She thrives on consistency and isn't quick to change, not even in stress. Contention and stress simply make her want to withdraw and allow things to settle; then, she'll come out of hiding. Because she is non-confrontational, she needs an atmosphere of peace, contentment, and happiness. Even though Air people make the best friends for her, she will sometimes wonder if they are genuine and may not fully trust them until a lot of time passes. She trusts Earth, can be threatened and intimidated by Fire but loves other Water people.

Strategy

You may have mistaken your Water wife's cool demeanor for not caring at all or apathy. It is just that she is and prefers to be mellow and easy-going. It is almost as if she doesn't care about too much of anything, but she does.

Find out what your Water Wife's "Flow" is. In other words, find out what the normal and comfortable style and the pace is for her. Your Water wife needs her flow to be maintained at all costs. Taking her outside, it means there will be problems when it comes time to produce. She is motivated but shows it with slow, consistent, and lasting habits. She will support you and help without demanding to be seen and heard. This is perfect if you are a Fire or Air husband. If you patiently and calmly lead her, explaining what needs to be done and why this silent rock will consistently support and work to accomplish what you want. Remember, once her waters are stirred, she won't forget the turmoil you caused or the agitation you keep stirring up. You must calmly and gently surf these still waters.

Take A Moment

Take a look at the kind of person you need from your wish list and compare what you have with what's on your list. With stress, you may have to help out a little.

Here is where you come to the rescue. Look at your wife's element, ask yourself what she needs and wants, and ask yourself what you can do to make that happen for her. In stress, she needs you. She can work on change later; in stress, she needs comfort.

Sex and Personality

Sex is a part of marriage, and each element has its own sexual personality that if partners understood, this could lead to greater fulfillment in the area of intimacy. Needs are best met when they are understood; many sexual issues in marriage are simply a lack of understanding of the personality traits as it relates to the sexual needs of the other person. We will not only look at each personality's strengths but their sexual and intimate characteristics.

Earth Strengths
This gets a little tricky. Your Earth wife seems to be very methodical and, at times, almost withdrawn. What his hiding beneath the surface is a molten core of passion, just like the planet itself. This may be disguised in many ways. Your Earth wife may want to pencil in time for romantic and sexual activity. She realizes it's not a time for studying charts and graphs or calculating how to please you. It's just that she feels better if she is prepared. Her strength is in research and planning. That is where the issue comes in. Intimacy and sexuality are romantic and spontaneous

by nature. The encounter has to be naturally come about and not calculated. She is smart enough to know that certain atmospheres and settings are "sexy" and may lead to sex. She thinks in terms of being ready for the encounter. Looking ahead as she often does, if she doesn't think she is ready, she may shy away from the setting or outing that she thinks will lead to sex.

You know that your Earth wife has an emotional and physically intimate side. Given the complex makeup of her personality and style, she simply needs to know what is required, expected, and acceptable. You won't get wild spontaneity from her, but you will be pleased with her unleashed passion. Comfort is key for her in any area of expression.

Knowing what is about to take place, she likes to set the mood in preparation and so she will really plan it out, perhaps with candles, music, flowers, and lots of romance. She can comply with your wishes and be glad to do so, knowing it is emotionally and physically fulfilling your needs. Not much for words, you can rest assured that whatever she says, it has taken some effort, honesty, and desire. To the Earth Personality, talking about intimacy can be as serious a deal as spending money when things are tight.

Your Earth wife likes to demonstrate what she thinks, feels, and wants when it comes to intimacy. In her mind, why say it when you can demonstrate it. Keep in mind, all of this is depending on her being comfortable and in the moment. She isn't talkative, so don't say something that will through her off; just follow her lead. When she knows that you are catering to her, she may even show extra effort as a kind of thank you. She quietly imagines certain sexual acts with you that wouldn't be fantasies but rather unspoken desires. Being with you intimately gives her a sense of comfort and satisfaction because she knows she can count on you, and respects that you accept and appreciate what she has to offer.

Part of her is willing to take tiny baby steps toward experiencing something new with you, but not too fast. She needs to take things at her own pace. She needs time to read or research some of the new things you might want to try. Again, go at her own pace.

In Intimacy

Think of the Earth as it slowly travels around the sun, taking months to complete a cycle. This is similar to your Earth wife going through a full week, or even a month, simply to get to a place where everything is safe and comfortable to share the intimacy she has been storing. With a cool, calm way about her, she is able to say to herself, "I'll get around to that..." Don't worry, just as she can rattle off to you what you said a week ago in a discussion; she is able to remember all that she desires to do with you intimately. She is yet curious about certain parts of you.

She understands the world and life but hasn't completely figured you out yet. Meaning she is uncertain or even confused about something you said, did, or even a particular trait of yours on some level. You can rest assured that there is something about your personality or habits that she would like to tweak. What you will get out of her is what she is sure of. She is confident because she has been thinking about it for a long time and has taken notes on what not to do or say. In intimacy, she certainly has taken her notes. She has been studying You. Because she has standards and expectations, she is pleased with a large part of who you are. She won't tell you or share her whole heart with you all at once, no matter how much she trusts you. This is why you must pay attention to her intimate side, hearing what she doesn't say. Let her actions and passions speak to you. Secrecy is the power to her, for some strange reason. In intimacy, she trusts the person who will genuinely care about her, which must be proven through time. She trusts the person that is honest and consistent in their habits and communications. This is the person that wins the key to her secrets.

Depending on her appetite for intimacy, you may discover there is much more to your Earth wife than you ever knew. It's worth having a discussion about it.

Sex

In marital intimacy, the experience is much like the Earth Personality itself. On the Earth's surface, you experience many different climates based on where you are, but the molten core is always hot. On the outside, she seems to be cautious if not rigid and uninviting and giving a little dry humor every now and then. However, the core of the person you engage with is quite the opposite. The Earth Personality has a great deal of passion and desire that may need expression more than the words she may want to speak but doesn't. Depending on her comfort level, she will be more apt to express herself sexually than verbally. Earth is not really a hard nut to crack but is just as true to the analogy. Your wife's outside is difficult to break, but the inside, her mind, heart, and soul are soft and inviting.

Having broken through the shell and engaging the intimate Earth Personality, there are moments when your Earth wife let's go to enjoy the experience without judgment or apprehension. You will see that some of her most enjoyable moments are found in her natural expressions and moments where her responses have not been calculated. That is when you get a true picture of the depth of her beauty, pure and simple. Your Earth wife usually thinks herself in and out of trouble. However, in moments of deep intimacy and transparency, she flows freely from the heart, and it is a beautiful thing to see.

As wonderful as things may be in the bedroom, remember she is a realist to her heart. When it's over, and its business as usual, she may be a little ashamed or even feel vulnerable that she let her deepest heart and feelings out in the open. Part of her is reserved for the "What If" of future betrayal and rejection. This is why you must continue to nurture a comfortable atmosphere for her to express herself freely.

Strategy
Your Earth wife is a treasure worth waiting for. If you can weather the occasional pessimism, doubt, or cynicism, you gain the best of both worlds in your Earth wife. Like her Fire cousin, you have to work with her from the inside out. The Earth wife is analytical, calculating, and often reads between the lines. Your strategy should always be one of honesty and transparency, even though she may be hesitant at first to be the same way to you. She is making up her mind if she should fully share her secret self while taking notes to see if you are consistent and trustworthy. She may have married you but will operate with you on a safe and calculated basis. This is just her way of being and dealing with reality. To her, the world is a scary place filled with uncertainty everywhere, in the most comfortable places like your arms. To her, "You never know what someone might do..." Winning her heart and trust is an achievement. Be proud of yourself for doing so.

To boost your sex-life, understand that she needs to talk about what pleases her at her own level of transparency. Chances are, you may never get to the deepest core or level of all she wants sexually. Take time to provide a comfortable and nurturing atmosphere where she can share without judgment or you overreacting. Remember her sensitive side and cynical tongue.

~

Air Strengths

We have discussed Air's attributes and how it is light, free-hearted, lively, and the life of the party. That being said, your Air wife can be the life of the party in a crowd or just with you. Her strength is in her ability to express what she is thinking and feeling shameless. Her expressions and the life she brings can be fun, even in intimacy. There is no shame in her game, if it's fun, she has the room for it.

Verbal intimacy can be dangerous ground for your Air wife, but really for you. When she wants to, she has the ability to speak and ignite desire and passion, as well as paint an intimate picture your mind would love. She is powerful. Her strength to communicate and express in words of poetry or straight from the heart is amazing. Her ability to communicate is only topped by her ability to let loose and passionately demonstrate her desires.

In Intimacy

In intimacy, your Air wife has to pull away from the fun of the moment and begin to experience you selflessly. Since Air loves to be the center of attention, they love receiving attention. This translates to a love of affection when it comes to intimacy. The Air

Personality has to become more aware of what the other person is feeling and wishes to say. Air makes the mistake of thinking that the moment is about them, and sharing becomes a chance to talk about themselves. Like opening Pandora's box and never being able to return, the Air Personality can begin sharing and hardly ever stop. It is their love of communication and sharing that opens the floodgates and will sweep the entire moment away if allowed.

Your Air wife lives to ride the wave of the moment. She is spontaneous, willing, and affirming. Stepping closer to the wild side, she may willingly open her heart and mouth just to see what she will say and do. She can be a chance taker and risk seeing what happens. Just know that at that moment, that is what she wanted to do even though it may change later. She is intuitive and may be able to lead the conversation or may feel she needs to explore a completely new area. With her, she is best when she feels free to express and explore without judgment. Remember, she needs acceptance and wants to know that she can express herself without getting into a debate that ruins the mood. Just as the wind dances and moves where it wills, she needs you to be open and free, ready to experience new things, verbally and physically. She loves being open and free with sharing and may even be a little of an exhibitionist who wants to show her curves to you. Like the wind itself, the Air Personality is unpredictable when it comes to what they may be thinking and feeling. As she shares her feelings, sharing can give her a "high" or sense of satisfaction. The only thing that is more enjoyable to her is receiving what she gives to you. Because she likes spontaneity and adventure, she wants you to surprise her with new things, different conversations, and daring actions. The last thing she wants is to be bored in romance and the bedroom with the same old routine time after boring time.

Sex

Your Air wife can be very expressive when it comes to physical intimacy. She wants physical intimacy that is spontaneous, different, and of course, fun. Whatever was done on the floor, she might want to try from the ceiling. Whatever was done laying down, she may want to try standing up. She needs variety and change. Again, boredom is not her thing.

That said, she may be willing to explore many new things with you, if you're game. And yes, to her, a game is just that, a game. She has no problem being true to you but wants to see and experience different sides of your sexuality. Because she is expressive, she may not mind telling you exactly what she wants and how many times she wants it. If you give her a chance, she will even come up with ideas and changes in the bedroom for you to say yes to. Just ask Air the simple question, "What do you want to do..." and they will let you know. Don't be surprised if they suggest an idea or a place that you never thought of.

Remember, your Air wife wants to be noticed, accepted and admired by you. You should try to make her feel welcome and free to express herself sexually. You are the only partner she has, and she needs to know that you are able to build your sexual relationship without judgment, with freedom, laughter, and a sense of fun. This means that Air will try to please to receive the needed level of acceptance. Your Air wife wants to be all that you will ever need and loves to hear your truthful and honest praise and acceptance. Air is open to a physically intimate moment and is usually accepting of anything enjoyable and fun. With Air, you have a fun and exciting relationship that will always give you something fresh and new. Your Air wife is always ready to enjoy the fun with the one she loves.

As a man, much of our sexuality is mental. Sometimes we think of our performance and may become insecure if we see that we have a challenge or two. With your Air wife, she is understanding and wants you to let go of the need to perform, and simply enjoy the intimate moment with her. We tend to judge ourselves based on a number of things, such as whether she screams, screams, climaxes, or just say thanks afterward. She, on the other hand, like many of her sisters, is just happy to have an intimate physical moment with the one she loves. The intimacy itself is worth it to her. So, relax and enjoy the moment and stop judging yourself.

Strategy

The Air wife that you have may make you wonder why she dresses a little snazzy just to go to the grocery store. You may wonder why she talks so freely and jokes with people she doesn't even know. What may also be of concern is how she seems to purposefully seek the attention of male and female bystanders. Your wife is full of life, love, and laughter. She only wants to share her joy for life with others because that's who she is, a breath of fresh are to everyone she meets. That is one of the first things you noticed and liked about her. She is still this way, but you are the one that caught her eye and her heart. You don't need to worry. What she needs from you is a playmate that will have fun, or make things fun, while keeping her grounded to Earth. She needs balance. To her, acceptance and affirmation mean a lot. Her heart rejoices in the fun but is comforted by everything being in order. In order, she can relax and enjoy the moment rather than panic. The challenge is you may be providing a majority of the order she needs. Since Air has no problems with physical or emotional intimacy, you can maintain the fun by being her partner in passion, conversation, and is a reminder that being grounded is a safe place to be.

She is expressive. Have an open and candid conversation with her about your deepest desires, and she will do the same for you. Be open to new things, try something new in foreplay, and see if you can spark a new experience. She will appreciate your understanding of her needs.

Fire Strengths

Did I mention that Fire burns hot? Well, if I didn't, it does, especially in the area of intimacy and romance. Since your Fire wife is usually busy, she may never feel as if she has enough time to complete all her tasks and plan her plans, which include you. Remember, your Fire wife is driven by winds of passion, progress, and principles. She has a high moral idea of how she should operate. When it comes to you, there are many passions and desires that she can think of.

She will often turn a purely innocent observation into a sexual or intimate idea for fun. Fun and funny, and the same time, it also serves as a hint of what may be in store tonight or in a few minutes. She is full of fire and passion and doesn't have a problem showing you just how hot her fire burns.

As verbal intimacy goes, she doesn't need a lot of conversation. She says what she wants to say and waits to see if her desires will be pursued or acted upon. Remember, your Fire wife can sum up situations, read people, and intuitively see when a moment is ready for action or just be patient. This also includes you.

Not to say that she will hit the nail on the head every time, but she will certainly read you and your readiness to play. At that moment, when she has pulled away from all of the world's concerns, you become her only project for the moment.

Her power of observations, passion, and desire for progress, causes her to focus her talents and powers on the task at hand. She is able to do many things with her abilities, and she would like to know that you share her dream and passion for progress, especially if it involves only you and her. Don't forget that she is inspired by a vision, which comes easy for her. This includes a vision of you and her in a romantic and intimate setting. She has the power to bring things to pass.

In Intimacy

In intimacy, this power translates into a deep, powerful, and sensuous passion. The only trick is to get the Fire to stop burning on a task, project, or her crusade to save the world, long enough to burn in your direction. But rest assured that it will.

The Fire wife has a short fuse when it comes to igniting her passion for intimacy. Just as quickly as she can be motivated to take on a project or the world, she could be equally quick to come knocking on your door of intimacy and expect action.

Fire personalities have respect for words and the languages that use them. They are usually good communicators and can be quite convincing. This means they make great romance partners and masters of verbal intimacy. Because they live in a world of passion and emotion, they really know how to captivate the heart (when they want to). Fire lives in a world of conviction, reason, and passion. Think of this as her having her own "Air" supply, which feeds her internal flame. Fire considers Air Personalities to be a slice of heaven because they are equally engaging, passionate, and inspirational. Fire needs these ingredients to remain passionate. These passions are just as powerful as she is and can sway her in one direction or another.

As powerful as Fire is, she lives or dies by the amount of "Air" her mate shares with her, or that she can self-generate. Her passions may be many. She is able to remain moral and upright as long as she doesn't develop a mindset where the "ends justify the "means." Her being task-oriented follows her everywhere and involves everything. When she puts her mind to a task, it's the only thing that matters. "I'll give you a hug later after I finish - I'm busy right now." Later, she will come to herself when the moment is right, and she will allow intimacy.

You never know when your Fire wife will say something that hits you right in the heart. She can be just as emotionally powerful as she is effective. Her ability to light you on Fire is only as powerful as her appetite for love and affection.

Sex

If she is convinced the timing is right, then she is ready for physical intimacy. Because her world is one of domination and controlling things, she may revert to a more passive lover, allowing you to take the lead. This also serves her because she wants to accomplish the task of pleasing you. As you might imagine, the power and strength of her ability to make things happen to give her the determination to be a great partner both physically and emotionally. Sexually, she is given to spontaneity and may get "turned on" at the drop of a hat. She may prefer quick sessions that relieve unwanted stress and tension. For her, there doesn't have to be a special reason or moment.

Each of the personality types has a second element or combination. The passion and desire of a Fire Personality will be adjusted accordingly. For element combinations, you may want to review them in "Mastering Your Personality" volumes one and two. If not, there is enough information here to get a decent understanding. If your wife is a pure Fire wife (meaning she doesn't have a second or third combination to her personality like 'Fire-Water, or Fire-Air,' etc.), she may want to control the intimate moment as well fully. A pure Fire wife has no problem telling you exactly what she wants in the bedroom.

Your Fire wife may be just as impatient in the bedroom as she is in areas. She has to live and love at the speed of thought and expectation. This is what she would like to do but doesn't always get to. Remember how she drives, as if she's always in a hurry. She wants to get to the point of intimacy and climax with purpose, even if it's just to cuddle afterward and savor the moment.

Strategy

Connect with her deeper by having intimate conversations with her about her passions and desires as it relates to what she wants in life, who she really is inside, and her vision for herself and her family. Throw in a little fiery boldness and say something sexy that she doesn't expect, and the intimacy game is on. I heard it said that If a man is in love with a woman's body, then any woman's body will do. However, if he has learned to love his woman's soul, then only she will do. You want to deepen the connection you have with her by touching the "Air" in her. Think of her Fire as the result of "Air" working in him. Take away your emotion, passion, visions, and dreams of the future, and she becomes a frustrated and ineffective partner. She is result-oriented and does appreciate progress. But remember, her desired progress is only wanted because of her desires, visions, and dreams.

~

Water Strength

Water with a match? Let me tell you; it just doesn't work. That is why springing an intimately sexual surprise on your Water wife isn't a good idea. It is not uncommon for the Water Personality to continue in their normal, mildly happy routine and suddenly be shocked by request for verbal or physical intimacy. This usually just doesn't work for her. If she is feeling generous, she may comply just to please you and make everything alright. If unprepared, your Water wife will need a moment to get with the program. For Water, method and consistency are important. The conversation leading to verbal or physical intimacy isn't welcome if there hasn't been consistent kindness and affection. Water wants to continue in its path of predictable.

Intimacy in communication is important, but not as important as honesty and trustworthiness. Water wants any conversation of a serious nature to be slow and non-offensive. More sensitive to body language and changes in vocal tones, Water feels what is being communicated. Water not only looks at what is being said but the way it is being said. Intimacy allows Water to listen and decide if the train of thought fits for the moment. To your Water wife, the intimate conversation begins long before you say, "I want to talk..." She looks at the pattern of conversations and your normal way of communicating things. Your Water wife is convinced of your love and dedication by what you continually say and not what you say in the heat of the moment. This is why she can overlook a few things said in the heat of an argument. The only problem with this is, if you consistently insult, belittle, or say the wrong thing, it becomes established as truth that you don't care or appreciate them much. You don't want that. Consistency and kindness are key. She will understand that you care by seeing your consistency.

In Intimacy

Your Water wife is, by nature, an emotional being. This brings new meaning to the saying, "Still waters run deep." The depth of these still waters is the depths of emotion. She feels a lot even though she may not say it until the time is right. This is why she is pleased to feel the love and warmth provided. Warmth and gentleness must accompany any desire that will become physical. She doesn't like any sudden rushing when it comes to verbal or physical intimacy. Again, think of your Water wife as a great body. Of Water that you have to move by yourself. If you are going to be successful, you have to be very slow and methodical with her, patience rules. You can't just move Water the way you want without causing damage. Water never wants to be moved suddenly; she wants things to flow the way she wants to go.

Sex

Intimacy has to be planned and prepared for. This is why physical intimacy usually is a planned activity that is part of a special occasion like a birthday, anniversary, or even a holiday. Water Personality likes to take their time and enjoy the experience, especially because it may be a while before it comes around again.

It might be a good idea to notice how Water and Earth have similar traits, just like Fire and Air does. Just as Earth needs to plan and be prepared for the sexual moment, your Water wife has to gradually flow into the passionate moment. Flow is important to her. Water has no problem with the planned and expected moment of physical intimacy. As in their normal everyday life, they may ask, "How may I help you..." Water enjoys the experience but doesn't mind being there for the other person.

Your Water wife is pleased with the opportunity to please you. On the other hand, Water may be reluctant to tell you what they want or even expect in the moment of physical intimacy. Just like the Water Personality can lead when given the proper tools and information, the same applies in the bedroom. Don't expect her to just swing from the chandelier with spontaneity and creativity. She is dependable and is consistent and can be easily accommodated. Unlike Air, she doesn't require a lot of change in the bedroom. Sure, she doesn't mind a little variety every now and then, but for the most part, she needs something she can count on, and that's you.

Strategy

With your Water wife, sex can be like a mortgage payment; it should come once a month and keep you living comfortably for a while. To the other personality types (except Earth), that simply won't do. Water may want physical intimacy more than usual if there is a secondary personality type. Find out what your Water wife's second personality type is and play to that. As a Water Personality, intimacy must be planned out and taken slowly and methodically. Don't rush. If you rush Water, you ruin the moment and maybe even more moments to come. Realize that you have a gentle and faithful partner that loves to help, even with intimacy. She needs you to care enough about intimacy with her to plan for it, start days in advance, to create the flow for it, and not just spring it on her. Take your time and be patient. Speak with your Water wife and find out not only what she likes and wants but also what turns her on.

Even a conversation like this has to be grown from one intimate and expressive conversation to another. You have to be patient in dealing with your Water wife. If you remember that it's not a race but a journey with her, you will do well.

Take A Moment

Is the sexual relationship with your wife really about her or about you? If you imagine the feeling you will get from sex instead of doing what it takes to make her feel a certain way, then it's about you and not her. Chances are she's satisfied only some of the time. Consider making her the number one focus in the bedroom by reflecting on the following two points:

1. What are some ways you can do this based on her personality? If you have been with her more times than you can count and still do not know what she likes or how she likes it, it has been

about you and not about her. Take more time during foreplay to rediscover what she likes and how she likes it.
2. If her not reaching a climax doesn't bother you, then it is certainly about you and not about her. Even if she says, "that's okay," you should still make things right by her no matter what. In the bedroom, you should dedicate yourself to pleasing her. How often do you do this?

Chapter 6
Loving Your Wife Without the But

> "Love your spouse more than you love your career, hobbies, and money. That stuff can never love you back anyway."
> - **Unknown**

When you consider the interesting mix of personalities within one person, you could find a world of mystery in every person you meet. For instance, it is not uncommon to find a Fire-Water personality type where the coping and harmony producing skills and habits are built automatically into the person's way of thinking and living. However, when it comes to putting a Fire personality type with a Water personality type, things may not flow as smoothly.

Why is that? One reason is that we have lost the ability to communicate with each other on a deeper level, a level that gets to the heart of the person and the heart of the matter. I am talking about a level of communication that is love-based, heartfelt, and truly nurturing. I am not talking about a communication that blames the other person or justifies another. I'm talking about truth that deepens our understanding and love for each other.

For reasons that I just mentioned, I've seen many things in relationships: like a Water person that can't get along with their Earth-Water mate even though it was the Water in them that attracted them to each other. You would think the Water personality would have common ground to stand on and mend any issues within the relationship. It didn't work at first for a very strong reason: communication.

Communication

As we look at the links of this chain, communication is first and should never be forgotten or neglected. Couples often skip communicating with each other for the sake of keeping the peace, saving time, or just not wanting to open a can of worms. I've found that not to communicate makes peace impossible, kills a lot of time, and turns a can of worms into a barrel of snakes. In other words, it makes things a lot worse

Take A Moment

Consider the following areas of your communication about your relationship and about your partner.

1) You have unspoken desires, frustrations, and issues with your wife that must be ironed out if

you intend to find and keep happiness in your marriage relationship.

2) What you say to your guy-friends should be easily said to your wife, who should be your best friend and communicated with more intimately than your guy-friends. If you are speaking more truthfully to them than your wife, you are more intimate with your guy-friends than your own spouse. Don't let it happen, or don't let it continue.

3) The only way to cross this bridge of communication is to start opening your mouth, lovingly but truthfully, always being true to who you are.

Fear

Somewhere along the way, we have been made to feel afraid to show who we really are. This includes showing others our secrets. If they knew we liked a certain thing or desired a certain thing, they wouldn't like us. Because we value affirmation more than direction, we put on the mask to be liked by others - including our mates.

Take A Moment

Consider embracing the following suggestions around fear.

1) Gently but boldly walk away from your fear of being rejected by the one you married - be yourself without apology.
2) Stop being afraid of your wife's differences and find a place for every attribute and habit your wife has. There is a place for them in your life, and they have the purpose of making you a better, stronger man.
3) Lovingly communicate what you need and stop being afraid to hurt her feelings. She can take it if you tell her in love.
4) Stop being afraid she will leave you or not love you anymore. I have found that heart to heart conversations create more love and trust. I've seen people get closer through loving communication.

Married And Settling

If you are married and feel things won't get any better regardless of what you do, then you are suggesting marriage doesn't work and that it's better to live in a lie than to live the truth. This isn't true, and you don't have to settle.

Take A Moment

Be honest with yourself, do you want to live a life of settling? You don't have too.

1) All the reasons you fell in love with your wife still exist. The only thing is you've had a lot more of it, so it feels familiar. Take the list of reasons you fell in love with your wife from the earlier chapters and go out on a date with your wife. Purposely focus on and appreciate those things.
2) Find out something new about your wife each month or week and add that to what you didn't know. Such conversations can start by you asking questions like, "What was your most embarrassing moment, happy moment, craziest thing you ever did, …etc."
3) Find something to compliment her on every single day.
4) Try to thank her more often.
5) Try to see things from her perspective before opening your mouth to say one word.
6) Set out to participate with her in her "moments" where she's doing something that annoys you.
7) Lastly, realize that every part of her was made for you and that she is responding to you based on how she's wired. She loves you.

This last chapter includes observations for you to take a moment and consider. I want to be intentional with encouraging you to learn to love what you feel you hate about your mate. In this book, I have uncovered and explored the depths of your personality, your wife's personality, and sought to draw you closer through deeper communication, understanding, and even helping you to see that she is all you really need. Everything that you want in a woman is there. The way you access the treasures is to understand her personality and work with her. You will never get what you are after by fighting her for it. You need to work with, not against her.

Finally, one of the greatest gifts this book offers is the chance to see her in a "New" light. She isn't the same old woman, wife, or girl. She is a living, breathing, endless source of life, love, and adventure. She has so much more waiting for you to draw out of her.

Be encouraged. If you've paid attention to the content of this book, you are well on your way to a deeper and more loving relationship than before. I wrote this book with both you and your wife in mind. So relax, if you guys are in this together – she's learning more about you too. The love you've always wanted is the love you can have. While it may not happen overnight, that's okay – you have a lifetime together to experience it.

Love your wife without the buts.

Next Steps

For coaching or to connect with Robert Pyles, visit rpthebig6.com

You may also invite Robert Pyles to speak by sending an email to pastorpyles@yourabundantfaith.org

Other Titles by Robert Pyles
Anchoring the Big 6

With over 20 years of experience as an Executive Coach, I've found that there are six primary areas in life that one must be anchored to experience exponential success in every area of their life. The Big 6 is not theory; it consists of proven principles to transform your life in Finance, Health, Relationships, Personal Development, Spiritual Growth, and Purpose. Before you make your next move, make sure you have mastered Anchoring The Big 6.

Coming Fall 2020
Mastering Your Personality Vol. I & II

www.ingramcontent.com/pod-product-compliance
Lightning Source LLC
Chambersburg PA
CBHW050323120526
44592CB00014B/2024